STUDY GUIDE

Anglo-Saxon and Norman England, c1060–88

Edexcel - GCSE

www.GCSEHistory.com

Published by Clever Lili Limited.

contact@cleverlili.com

First published 2020

ISBN 978-1-913887-13-1

Copyright notice

All rights reserved. No part of this publication may be reproduced in any form or by any means (including photocopying or storing it in any medium by electronic means and whether or not transiently or incidentally to some other use of this publication) with the written permission of the copyright owner. Applications for the copyright owner's written permission should be addressed to the publisher.

Clever Lili has made every effort to contact copyright holders for permission for the use of copyright material. We will be happy, upon notification, to rectify any errors or omissions and include any appropriate rectifications in future editions.

Cover by: DeFacto on Wikimedia Commons

Icons by: flaticon and freepik

Contributors: Marcus Pailing, Helen Lamb, Shahan Abu Shumel Haydar, Jen Mellors

Edited by Paul Connolly and Rebecca Parsley

Design by Evgeni Veskov and Will Fox

All rights reserved

DISCOVER MORE OF OUR GCSE HISTORY STUDY GUIDES

GCSEHistory.com and Clever Lili

  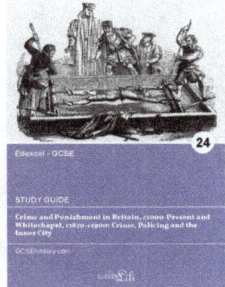 

THE GUIDES ARE EVEN BETTER WITH OUR GCSE/IGCSE HISTORY WEBSITE APP AND MOBILE APP

GCSE History is a text and voice web and mobile app that allows you to easily revise for your GCSE/IGCSE exams wherever you are - it's like having your own personal GCSE history tutor. Whether you're at home or on the bus, GCSE History provides you with thousands of convenient bite-sized facts to help you pass your exams with flying colours. We cover all topics - with more than 120,000 questions - across the Edexcel, AQA and CIE exam boards.

Contents

How to use this book 6
What is this book about? 7
Revision suggestions 9

Timelines
Late Anglo-Saxon and Early Norman England 13

Anglo-Saxon Society
Population of England in 1060 14
The Anglo-Saxons 14
The Danelaw 16
The Power of the Anglo-Saxon King 16
Power in Anglo-Saxon Society 17
Anglo-Saxon Land 18
The Anglo-Saxon Army 19
Anglo-Saxon Law Enforcement 19
Wergild 20
The Anglo-Saxon Economy 21
The Anglo-Saxon Church 22

The Reign of Edward the Confessor and the Succession Crisis
Edward the Confessor 23
Earl Godwin 24
Earl Aelfgar 26
Rebellion in Northumbria Against Tostig 26

The Rival Claimants for the Throne
The Succession Crisis 27
Harold Godwinson 29
Harald Hardrada 33
Edgar Aetheling 34

The Norman Invasion
Viking Invasion, 1066 35
Battle of Gate Fulford, 1066 36
Battle of Stamford Bridge, 1066 36
Significance of the Viking Invasion 37
The Norman Threat 38
Battle of Hastings, 1066 38
Armies and Tactics at the Battle of Hastings 41

Establishing Control
The English Surrender of 1066 42
William's Rewards to His Followers 43
The Marcher Earldoms 44
Motte and Bailey Castles 45

Anglo-Saxon Resistance, 1068-1071
Rebellions Against William 47
Edwin and Morcar's Rebellion, 1068 47
Edgar Aetheling's Rebellion, 1069 49
The Harrying of the North, 1069-1070 51
Hereward the Wake and Rebellion, 1070-1071 52

Revolt of the Earls, 1075
The Earls' Revolt 53

William I and His Sons
William I 55
Robert Curthose 59
William Rufus 60
Bishop Odo 61

The Legacy of Resistance to 1077
The Normans and Land 62
Changes to Landholding Under the Normans 64

The Feudal System and the Church
The Feudal System 65
Exchanges in the Feudal System 66
Forfeiture 66
Tenants-in-Chief 67
Knights 67
The Norman Church 68

Norman Government
Changes to England Under the Normans 70
Norman Government 71
The Norman Sheriff 72
The Royal Forests 72
The Domesday Book 73

The Norman Aristocracy
Norman Culture 74
Norman Fashion 75
Norman Architecture 75
Norman Leisure 76
Norman Chivalry 76
Norman Christianity 76
Norman Attitudes to the Anglo-Saxons 77
Changes to Inheritance Laws Under the Normans 77
The Norman Language 77

Glossary 79

Quizzes, amazing exam preparation tools and more at GCSEHistory.com

Index 83

HOW TO USE THIS BOOK

In this study guide, you will see a series of icons, highlighted words and page references. The key below will help you quickly establish what these mean and where to go for more information.

Icons

WHAT questions cover the key events and themes.

WHO questions cover the key people involved.

WHEN questions cover the timings of key events.

WHERE questions cover the locations of key moments.

WHY questions cover the reasons behind key events.

HOW questions take a closer look at the way in which events, situations and trends occur.

IMPORTANCE questions take a closer look at the significance of events, situations, and recurrent trends and themes.

DECISIONS questions take a closer look at choices made at events and situations during this era.

Highlighted words

Abdicate - occasionally, you will see certain words highlighted within an answer. This means that, if you need it, you'll find an explanation of the word or phrase in the glossary which starts on **page 79**.

Page references

Tudor *(p.7)* - occasionally, a certain subject within an answer is covered in more depth on a different page. If you'd like to learn more about it, you can go directly to the page indicated.

WHAT IS THIS BOOK ABOUT?

Anglo-Saxon and Norman England, c1060-88 is a British depth study that investigates how England was ruled under the late Anglo-Saxons and the early Norman kings. The course focuses on the period from 1060 to the early reign of William Rufus in 1088. You will focus on crucial events during this period, and study the different social, cultural, political, economic and religious changes that occurred.

Purpose
This study will help you to understand the nature of Anglo-Saxon and Norman rule in England. You will investigate themes such as power, law and order, government, religion, and economy and society. This course will enable you to develop the historical skills of causation, consequence, importance, continuity, and change.

Topics
Anglo-Saxon and Norman England, c1060-88 is split into three key topics: Anglo-Saxon England and the Norman Conquest, 1060-66; William I in power: securing the kingdom, 1066-87; Norman England, 1066-88.

- Topic 1 looks at Anglo-Saxon society, the succession crisis in 1066, and the Norman invasion in 1066.
- Topic 2 looks at how William consolidated control after 1066. This includes how he dealt with Saxon rebellions against his rule, and how he faced a revolt by his own Norman followers in 1075.
- Topic 3 looks at how the Normans governed England. You will study the feudal system, the government and legal systems, and the Norman Church. Finally, you will learn about the accession of William Rufus, and the troubles he faced in the first years of his rule.

Key Individuals
Some of the key individuals studied on this course include:

- Edward the Confessor.
- Earl Godwin and his family.
- Harold Godwinson.
- Harald Hardrada.
- Edgar Aetheling.
- William I (William the Conqueror).
- Lanfranc, Archbishop of Canterbury.
- Bishop Odo of Bayeux.
- William II (William Rufus).
- Robert Curthose.

Key Events
Some of the key events you will study on this course include:

- The Battle of Stamford Bridge.
- The Battle of Hastings.
- The Saxon rebellions of 1067-1071.
- The Harrying of the North, 1069-70.
- The Earls' Revolt of 1075.
- The creation of the Domesday Survey.
- The accession of William Rufus, and the revolt against him by Odo of Bayeux.

Assessment
Anglo-Saxon and Norman England, c.1060-88 forms part of paper 2 which you have a total of 1 hour and 45 minutes to complete. You should spend around 50 minutes on this section of the paper. There will be three exam questions which will assess what you have learnt on the Anglo-Saxon and Norman England, c.1060-88 course.

- Question 1 is worth 4 marks. This question will require you to simply describe two features of an aspect of the course.
- Question 2 is worth 12 marks. This question will require you to explain the importance of a theme or event of the course by using your contextual knowledge. You will be given two prompts to indicate what you might include in your answer, but you must also use your own knowledge.

WHAT IS THIS BOOK ABOUT?

- Question 3 is worth 16 marks. You will have to choose one of two options. This question will require you to show your knowledge and understanding of the key features and characteristics of the course. You will have the opportunity to show your ability to explain and analyse historical events using second order concepts such as causation, consequence, change, continuity, similarity and difference. You will be given two prompts to indicate what you might include in your answer, but you must also use your own knowledge.

REVISION SUGGESTIONS

Revision! A dreaded word. Everyone knows it's coming, everyone knows how much it helps with your exam performance, and everyone struggles to get started! We know you want to do the best you can in your GCSEs, but schools aren't always clear on the best way to revise. This can leave students wondering:

- ✓ How should I plan my revision time?
- ✓ How can I beat procrastination?
- ✓ What methods should I use? Flash cards? Re-reading my notes? Highlighting?

Luckily, you no longer need to guess at the answers. Education researchers have looked at all the available revision studies, and the jury is in. They've come up with some key pointers on the best ways to revise, as well as some thoughts on popular revision methods that aren't so helpful. The next few pages will help you understand what we know about the best revision methods.

How can I beat procrastination?

This is an age-old question, and it applies to adults as well! Have a look at our top three tips below.

◎ Reward yourself

When we think a task we have to do is going to be boring, hard or uncomfortable, we often put if off and do something more 'fun' instead. But we often don't really enjoy the 'fun' activity because we feel guilty about avoiding what we should be doing. Instead, get your work done and promise yourself a reward after you complete it. Whatever treat you choose will seem all the sweeter, and you'll feel proud for doing something you found difficult. Just do it!

◎ Just do it!

We tend to procrastinate when we think the task we have to do is going to be difficult or dull. The funny thing is, the most uncomfortable part is usually making ourselves sit down and start it in the first place. Once you begin, it's usually not nearly as bad as you anticipated.

◎ Pomodoro technique

The pomodoro technique helps you trick your brain by telling it you only have to focus for a short time. Set a timer for 20 minutes and focus that whole period on your revision. Turn off your phone, clear your desk, and work. At the end of the 20 minutes, you get to take a break for five. Then, do another 20 minutes. You'll usually find your rhythm and it becomes easier to carry on because it's only for a short, defined chunk of time.

Spaced practice

We tend to arrange our revision into big blocks. For example, you might tell yourself: "This week I'll do all my revision for the Cold War, then next week I'll do the Medicine Through Time unit."

Get our free app at GCSEHistory.com

REVISION SUGGESTIONS

This is called **massed practice**, because all revision for a single topic is done as one big mass.

But there's a better way! Try **spaced practice** instead. Instead of putting all revision sessions for one topic into a single block, space them out. See the example below for how it works.

This means planning ahead, rather than leaving revision to the last minute - but the evidence strongly suggests it's worth it. You'll remember much more from your revision if you use **spaced practice** rather than organising it into big blocks. Whichever method you choose, though, remember to reward yourself with breaks.

Spaced practice (more effective):

week 1	week 2	week 3	week 4
Topic 1	Topic 1	Topic 1	Topic 1
Topic 2	Topic 2	Topic 2	Topic 2
Topic 3	Topic 3	Topic 3	Topic 3
Topic 4	Topic 4	Topic 4	Topic 4

Massed practice (less effective)

week 1	week 2	week 3	week 4
Topic 1	Topic 2	Topic 3	Topic 4

REVISION SUGGESTIONS

 What methods should I use to revise?

Self-testing/flash cards

Self explanation/mind-mapping

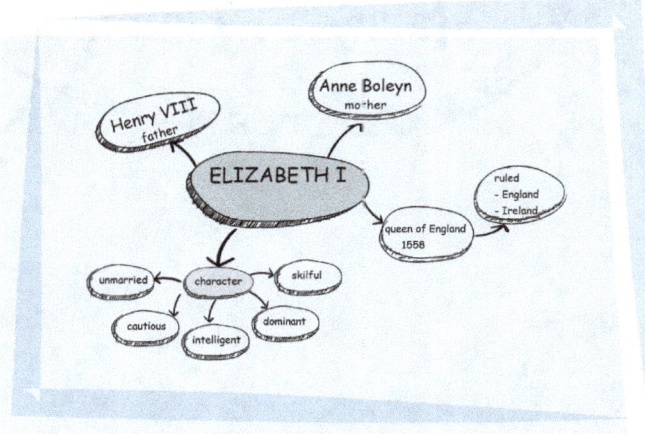

The research shows a clear winner for revision methods - **self-testing**. A good way to do this is with **flash cards**. Flash cards are really useful for helping you recall short – but important – pieces of information, like names and dates.

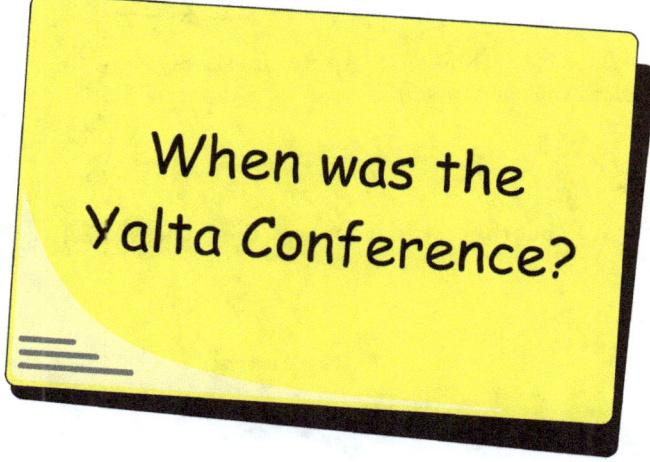

Side A - question

Side B - answer

Write questions on one side of the cards, and the answers on the back. This makes answering the questions and then testing yourself easy. Put all the cards you get right in a pile to one side, and only repeat the test with the ones you got wrong - this will force you to work on your weaker areas.

pile with right answers

pile with wrong answers

As this book has a quiz question structure itself, you can use it for this technique.

Another good revision method is **self-explanation**. This is where you explain how and why one piece of information from your course linked with another piece.

This can be done with **mind-maps**, where you draw the links and then write explanations for how they connect. For example, President Truman is connected with anti-communism because of the Truman Doctrine.

REVISION SUGGESTIONS

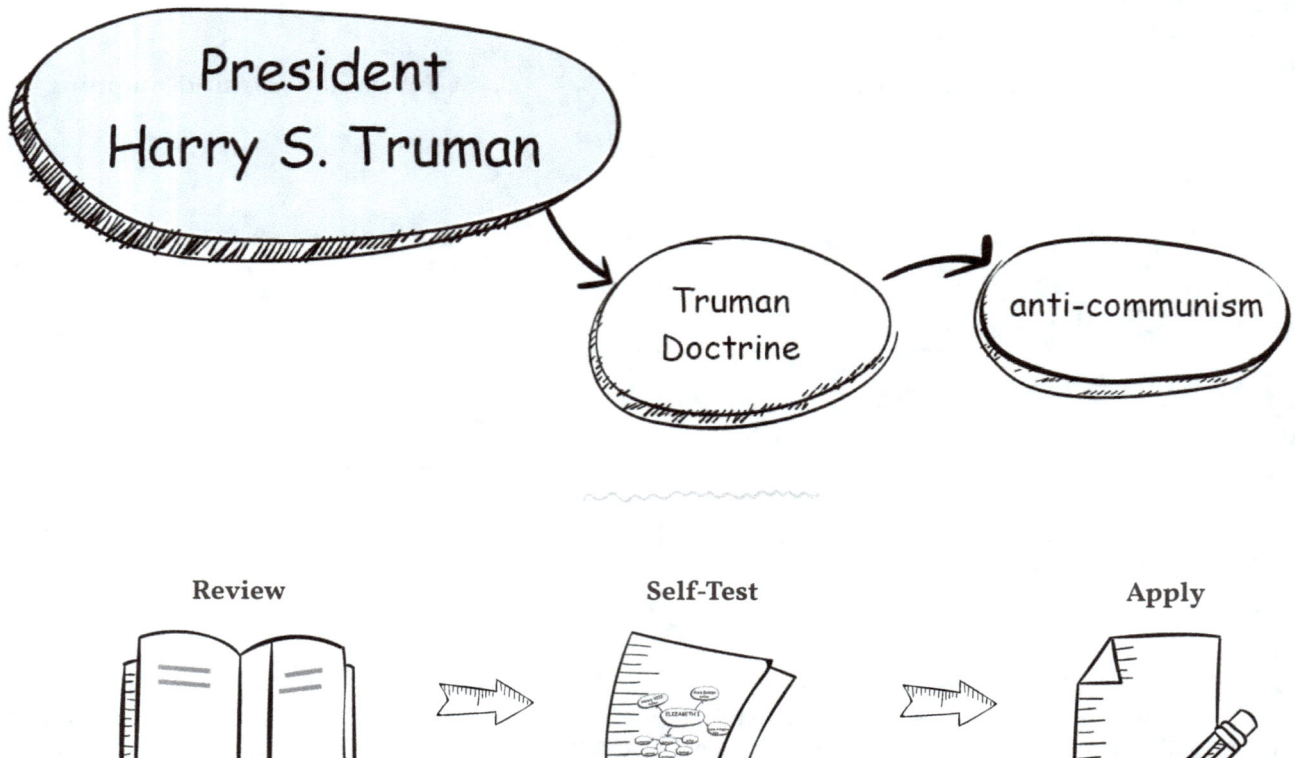

Review	Self-Test	Apply
Start by highlighting or re-reading to create your flashcards for self-testing.	Test yourself with flash cards. Make mind maps to explain the concepts.	Apply your knowledge on practice exam questions.

 ## Which revision techniques should I be cautious about?

Highlighting and **re-reading** are not necessarily bad strategies - but the research does say they're less effective than flash cards and mind-maps.

If you do use these methods, make sure they are **the first step to creating flash cards**. Really engage with the material as you go, rather than switching to autopilot.

LATE ANGLO-SAXON AND EARLY NORMAN ENGLAND

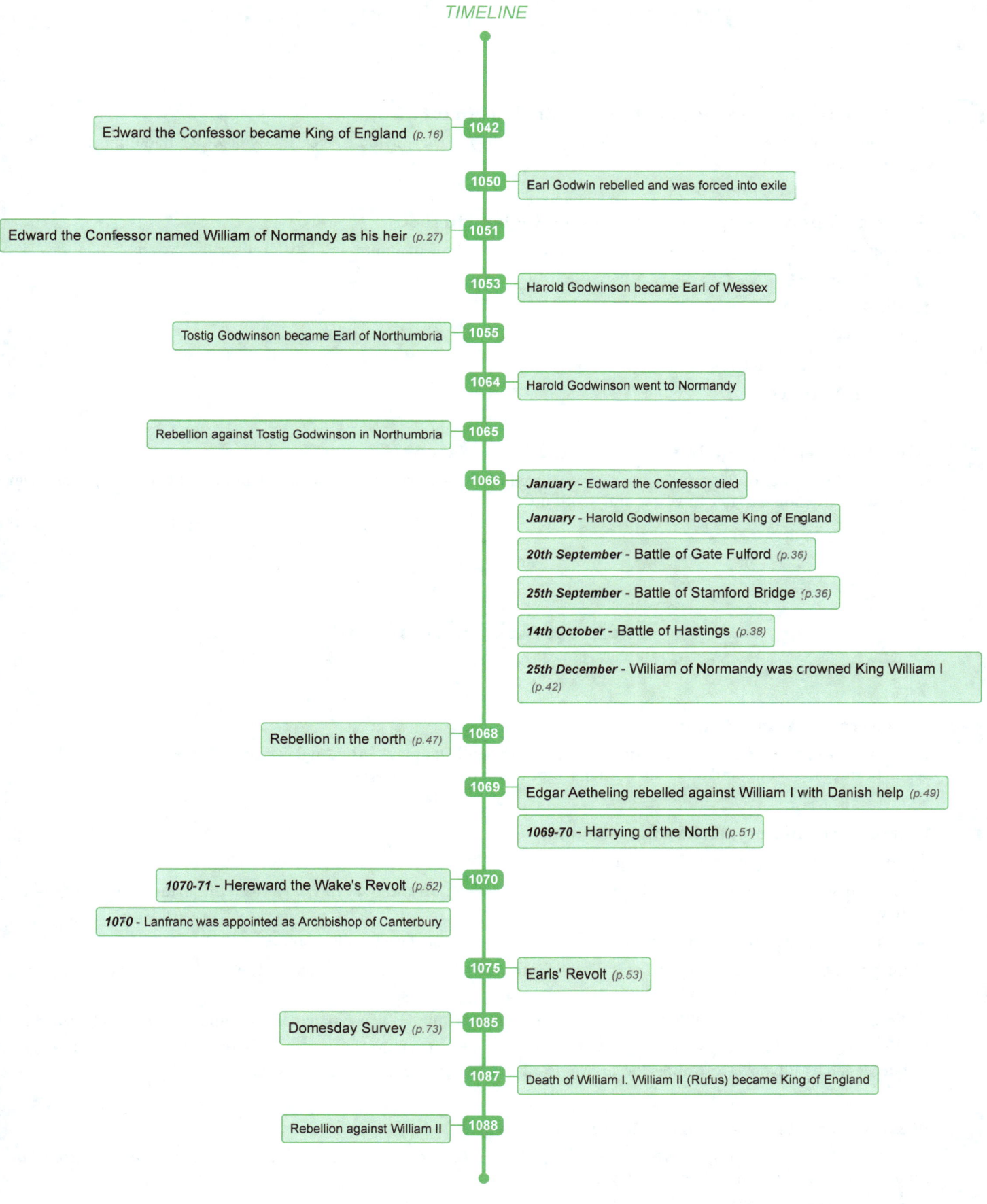

POPULATION OF ENGLAND IN 1060

An overview of the Anglo-Saxons, where they came from, and where they settled.

What groups made up the population of England in 1060?
There were a number of different groups in Britain during the early Middle Ages, many of which had migrated to the area from other countries.

Which groups made up the population of England in 1060?
The English population by 1060 was made up of the descendants of a number of different tribal groups.
- ✅ The Angles.
- ✅ The Saxons.
- ✅ The Jutes.
- ✅ The Ancient British tribes.
- ✅ The Anglo-Danes.

Who inhabited England in 1060 before the Anglo-Saxons?
Ancient British tribes of Picts and Celts were enslaved by the Anglo-Saxons when they migrated to Britain, or else were forced west and north to live in Wales and Scotland.

THE ANGLO-SAXONS

A brief history of Anglo-Saxon England and information on Anglo-Saxon society.

Who were the Anglo-Saxons?
The Anglo-Saxons were groups from northern Germany and Denmark - the Angles, the Saxons and the Jutes. They began to migrate to England after the Romans left Britain in around 400 AD.

What was the history of the Anglo-Saxons?
There were some key points in the history of the Anglo-Saxons.
- ✅ Around 600 AD they mass-converted to Christianity. Religion and the Church were an important feature of their lives.
- ✅ In around 800 AD the Vikings began to raid and invade areas of eastern England.
- ✅ Originally, Anglo-Saxon England was divided into seven kingdoms, known as the Heptarchy. After 937 AD these were united into one kingdom - England.
- ✅ From 1016-1035 the king of England was a Viking named Cnut. He was particularly popular in the Danelaw *(p. 16)*.
- ✅ Cnut was succeeded by two of his sons - Harold Harefoot and Harthacnut. When Harthacnut died in 1042 he was succeeded by Edward the Confessor, an Anglo-Saxon from the pre-Viking dynasty.

What was the Heptarchy in Anglo-Saxon England?
After 927 AD, the seven kingdoms of the Heptarchy remained as earldoms - large areas of land that were controlled on behalf of the king by rich and powerful warriors, called earls.
- ✅ Northumbria was in the north east of England.
- ✅ Wessex ran along the southern coastline of England, although the areas now known as Devon and Cornwall remained Celtic.

- Mercia covered most of the Midlands.
- East Anglia was on the east coast, below Northumbria.
- Essex, Sussex and Kent were located in the south east of England.

How was Anglo-Saxon society organised?

In Anglo-Saxon times, people in England lived in a social hierarchy. The most powerful and wealthy people at the top formed the aristocracy.

Who were the ceorls in Anglo-Saxon England?

Ceorls (also known as 'freemen') were free peasants who were not tied to the land, and who could leave to work for another lord if they chose.

Who were the peasants in Anglo-Saxon England?

Peasants made up the majority of Anglo-Saxon society. They rented small farms to support themselves and their families, and also worked for the local lord.

Who were the slaves in Anglo-Saxon England?

Slaves made up about 10% of Anglo-Saxon society. They could be bought and sold, like property.

Who were the thegns in Anglo-Saxon England?

Thegns were the local lords.

- They held more than 5 hides of land (about 600 acres).
- They lived in a manor house, sometimes with its own church.
- They were important people in the community, and rented their land to peasants.
- They formed the aristocracy in Anglo-Saxon society.

What did the earls do in Anglo-Saxon England?

The earls were:

- The most important, wealthy, and powerful men in Anglo-Saxon society.
- They had a relationship with the king that operated on trust, although they might challenge him to get more power.
- Overlords of the thegns, who fought in their armies.

How mobile was Anglo-Saxon society?

Although the status of Anglo-Saxon individuals depended on the importance of family and ancestors, their society was more flexible than others of the time. People could become more or less important within it.

- Thegns could be made into earls, and earls could be demoted to thegns.
- Peasants who gained and paid tax on more than five hides of land became thegns.
- Traders and merchants with their own ships could become thegns.
- Slaves could be freed by their masters.
- Peasants could sell themselves into slavery if they were desperate.

> **DID YOU KNOW?**
>
> The Anglo-Saxons spoke and wrote an early form of English, which we call either 'Anglo-Saxon' or 'Old English'. It neither looks nor sounds much like modern English, but is a direct ancestor of the language we speak today.

THE DANELAW

Although England was mostly Anglo-Saxon, large numbers of Viking settlers in the 9th century created the Danelaw in northern and eastern England.

 What was Danelaw?

The Danelaw was an area that covered the north and east of England during the 9th and 10th centuries. It was mainly controlled by the Vikings, and the Dane's law was used to rule the people (hence Danelaw).

 How were the Danelaw areas different to the rest of Anglo-Saxon England?

There were a number of differences between Danelaw and Anglo-Saxon England.

- ✔ The language *(p.77)* used in the Danelaw was different, with lots of Scandinavian words. For example, a hide was called a carucate.
- ✔ There were more ceorls (freemen) in the Danelaw, and peasants had more freedom to leave their lord's land.
- ✔ The amount of Danegeld payable, originally given as protection money to the Vikings, was much lower in the Danelaw.

> **DID YOU KNOW?**
>
> You can tell where different peoples settled in England through place names. Those in the area that was part of the Danelaw have Scandinavian elements which don't exist elsewhere.

THE POWER OF THE ANGLO-SAXON KING

The role and powers of the king in Saxon England.

 What did the king do in Anglo-Saxon society?

The king was the most important person in Anglo-Saxon society and fulfilled a number of roles.

 Who was the king of Anglo-Saxon England in 1060?

In 1060 the king of England was Edward the Confessor. He ruled from 1042 to 1066.

 Could the king make laws in Anglo-Saxon England?

Kings created 'Codes of Law' and distributed them through the country. The king was responsible for the 'King's Peace' and enforcing the laws overall, while the local lords and communities made sure that they were followed.

 How did the king control money in Anglo-Saxon England?

The king controlled the production of silver coins that were used as currency. Counterfeiting coins was a serious crime.

 How did the Anglo-Saxon king control land?

The king owned large portions of land and could grant it or take it away. Those who received it had to pay taxes and serve in the army.

How much control did the Anglo-Saxon kings have over the army?
The king could raise an army. Landowners had to bring and equip soldiers, or risk being fined or losing their land.

How did the king collect taxes in Anglo-Saxon England?
The king raised taxes through a national taxation system. He decided when taxes should be paid, and landowners had to pay or risk losing their land.

POWER IN ANGLO-SAXON SOCIETY

Although the king was the central authority in Anglo-Saxon England, others - the earls, the Witan and the shire reeves - held various powers.

Who held the power in Anglo-Saxon society?
Power in Anglo-Saxon was distributed through the hierarchy, with the most wealthy and important people at the top of society holding the most power and land.

What powers did the Anglo-Saxon kings have?
More than anything else, Anglo-Saxon kings needed a strong military force and a good army to maintain power.
- ✅ A reputation as a good warrior, and a history of winning battles, helped the king to maintain his power.
- ✅ Anglo-Saxons also respected a king who was an effective lawmaker and maintained the King's Peace.
- ✅ Kings could also earn respect by being pious and religious.

What limits were there on the king's power in Anglo-Saxon England?
Kings of England faced two main problems in maintaining control over the country.
- ✅ Half of the country was run by Anglo-Danes, who were descended from the Viking invaders. They used 'Danelaw (p.16)' in their areas, and preferred to rule themselves locally.
- ✅ Very powerful earls could present a problem. By 1060, some earls in England were so strong that they held more military power than the king.

What power did earls have in Anglo-Saxon England?
Earldoms were originally created after 1016 by the Viking King Cnut for his followers. However, they were soon passed on to important and trustworthy Anglo-Saxons.
- ✅ They collected taxes for the king, but were allowed to keep a third of all the money.
- ✅ They were supposed to use their wealth and power to maintain good order in their earldom.
- ✅ They oversaw law enforcement in their areas.
- ✅ They were lords to hundreds of thegns, and therefore had great military power.
- ✅ They kept small, private, highly-trained armies of housecarls for protection.

What limits were there on the earls' powers in Anglo-Saxon England?
Earls had a lot of economic, military and legal power, but their position was dependent on the king and their thegns.
- ✅ Earls had more power with a weak king on the throne, and were able to influence his decisions.
- ✅ A strong king demanded obedience and punished earls who disobeyed him.
- ✅ Thegns could demand that an earl should be demoted if they disliked the way that he ran their area.

What was the Witan in Anglo-Saxon England?

The Witan was the Anglo-Saxon government. It was a council made up of the most important men, and advised the king. The king appointed the Witan and decided when it should meet.

What did the Witan do in Anglo-Saxon England?

The Witan had 4 important roles.
- It advised the king on foreign threats and of possible wars.
- It discussed religious issues.
- It reached judgements in arguments about land.
- It played a role in choosing the new king.

What power did the shire reeve have in Anglo-Saxon England?

The shire reeve was the king's local official and represented his interests in his areas. Shire reeves later became known as sheriffs.
- They collected the geld tax on land that went directly to the king.
- They collected revenues from the king's own land.
- They collected fines from the shire court.
- They enforced the law in the shire.
- They oversaw the upkeep of roads and defences.
- They were responsible for providing men for the fyrd.

ANGLO-SAXON LAND

How the land was divided up in Anglo-Saxon England - from the shires to smaller land measurements, such as hides and hundreds.

How was Anglo-Saxon land divided up?

England was divided into around 34 shires, which were then divided into hundreds and then tithings. Each unit of land had its own responsibilities to the kingdom.

How was Anglo-Saxon land measured?

Anglo-Saxons land was divided into shires, hundreds and tithings.
- Shires later became known as counties. They had their own courts, provided troops for the fyrd, had a burh, and a king's representative in the form of the shire reeve.
- Hundreds were originally 100 hides of land, or areas that contained 100 families.
- Tithings traditionally contained ten families.

THE ANGLO-SAXON ARMY

The army in Anglo-Saxon England was made up of a professional core - the housecarls - and a mass of untrained levies - the fyrd.

 What soldiers were there in Anglo-Saxon England?
Anglo-Saxon England had two key types of soldiers: the fyrd and housecarls.

 What was the Anglo-Saxon fyrd?
The fyrd were the soldiers who went to fight in the king's army, if called upon. Each group of five hides had to provide one man for the fyrd, and the maximum term of service was 40 days.
- ✅ The fyrd were the soldiers who went to fight in the king's army, if called upon.
- ✅ The fyrd was disbanded after 40 days to make sure that men could return home to care for their farms and families.
- ✅ The select fyrd travelled England to fight for the king. These were usually well-trained, well-equipped thegns and their followers.
- ✅ The general fyrd was made up of men who fought only in their local area.
- ✅ By 1c60, communities could pay a fee instead of providing men for the fyrd. This could be used to hire soldiers instead.

 What type of soldier was a housecarl in Anglo-Saxon England?
Housecarls were well-trained, well-armed soldiers who acted as bodyguards for important nobles. They were the professional backbone of the army.

DID YOU KNOW?
It is said the strongest housecarls could chop off a horse's head with an axe - and go on to kill the man riding the horse - in one blow!

ANGLO-SAXON LAW ENFORCEMENT

Saxon law was sophisticated and effective, working on the principle of collective responsibility.

 How did Anglo Saxons enforce the law?
Law enforcement in Anglo-Saxon society relied heavily on the principle of collective responsibility.

 What was the role of the victims in Anglo-Saxon law enforcement?
Victims of crime were expected to find the criminal themselves.

 How did they catch criminals in Anglo-Saxon law enforcement?
The victim or witnesses were expected to call out to fellow villagers to assist in chasing the criminal. This was known as the hue and cry. If a person did not join in the chase the whole village would have to pay a heavy fine.

 Who were the Anglo-Saxon law enforcement officials?
Shire reeves were appointed from the local community to make sure people followed the king's law.

How did the Anglo-Saxon kings enforce the law?
There were 2 main ways the king enforced the law in Anglo-Saxon England:
- He was responsible for the 'King's Peace', which meant the people of Anglo-Saxon England held him ultimately responsible for protecting them and providing justice.
- Only the king could make laws, which were issued as Codes of Law. These might add new laws, or reinforce or change existing ones.

How was policing organised in Anglo-Saxon England?
Policing duties in Anglo-Saxon England were divided between the local community and the king's men in 2 key ways:
- The shire reeve acted on behalf of the king to make sure people followed the law.
- Local communities were divided into tithings to police each other. A tithing was a group of ten people.

How did tithings enforce the law in Anglo-Saxon England?
Tithings enforced the law in 3 different ways:
- The men of the tithing were responsible for the behaviour of everyone in the ten households.
- If someone saw a crime being committed, they had to raise a hue and cry by shouting so that anyone who heard could chase the criminal. Anyone who failed to do this had to pay a fine.
- If someone refused to join the fyrd, the whole tithing had to pay a fine.

WERGILD

Justice in Anglo-Saxon England was often obtained through the payment of fines which were calculated according the value of a person's life - the wergild.

What was wergild in Anglo-Saxon England?
Wergild replaced blood feuds as a method of obtaining justice in Anglo-Saxon England.

How was wergild used?
If someone was killed or injured, money called wergild would be paid to them or their family as compensation.

How much was wergild?
The amount of wergild was decided in the following 3 ways:
- The amount of wergild paid varied according to the crime.
- Lesser injuries cost less money than more serious ones.
- The status of the victim also affected the payment. For example, the cost of killing a thegn was much higher than the cost of killing a ceorl.

THE ANGLO-SAXON ECONOMY
The economy in Anglo-Saxon England, including towns and trade.

What was the Anglo-Saxon economy like?
The Anglo-Saxon economy was mostly based on farming, but some trading took place.

What was produced in the Anglo-Saxon economy?
It isn't clear what Anglo-Saxons produced for sale, but it is likely that there was a woollen cloth industry as the country was well-suited to sheep.
- Arable farming was easier in Anglo-Saxon England than in other parts of Europe.
- There were over 6,000 mills in the country for grinding grain into flour.

What money was used in the Anglo-Saxon economy?
The silver coins that were used in trading were strictly controlled by the king.
- They had to be a standard thickness and weight.
- The stamps that were used to make them were kept in one location that was controlled by the king.
- There were harsh punishments for counterfeiting (faking) coins.

What imports were in the Anglo-Saxon economy?
There is evidence that Anglo-Saxon England bought goods from other countries.
- Millstones and whetstones may have been bought from Denmark.
- Wine was purchased from Normandy.

How did towns help the Anglo-Saxon economy?
Towns were important centres of trade in Anglo-Saxon England. About 5% of the population lived in them by 1066.
- All trading above a certain amount, by law, had to be conducted in the burhs, so that the king could collect tax on it.
- The bigger towns tended to have international trading links.

Who did the Anglo-Saxon towns trade with in the economy?
Some towns in Anglo-Saxon England were centres of trade with other countries.
- London, which grew to 10,000 people, had trade links with Germany, France, Normandy and Flanders.
- York, which might had an estimated population of 9,000 people, traded with Denmark.

What was traded in the villages in the Anglo-Saxon economy?
Villages tended to consist of isolated farms, containing large extended families, with a manor house (and sometimes a church), built by the thegn.

THE ANGLO-SAXON CHURCH
The Christian Church in Anglo-Saxon England.

What role was played by the Church in Anglo-Saxon times?
The Church in Anglo-Saxon England was the Roman Catholic Church. Although there were lots of changes to the Church at this time, the Anglo-Saxon Church tended to stick to its familiar, traditional ways.

Who were bishops in the Anglo-Saxon Church?
Bishops ran large areas of the Church.
- They were often rich and powerful men.
- They might serve on the Witan.
- They sometimes clashed with thegns who built their own churches, as they wanted to keep control of priests and parishes.

Who were the priests in the Anglo-Saxon Church?
Priests worked in local churches.
- They were often just ordinary members of the community.
- They were often married, despite the Church's teachings on celibacy.
- They were often not very well-educated, and could not read Latin.

What were monasteries in the Anglo-Saxon Church?
Some Anglo-Saxons lived together in religious communities. These were known as monks and nuns, and lived in monasteries, abbeys and nunneries, run by abbots and abbesses.

How did the monasteries change in the Anglo-Saxon Church?
In 1060, the religious communities in Anglo-Saxon England were undergoing some changes.
- In Anglo-Saxon England, monasteries were in decline.
- Many Anglo-Saxon monasteries played a role in the local community, rather than staying separate and isolated.
- Because monasteries needed land, they had to rely on nobles to grant it to them. This led to complaints that the monasteries were under too much secular control.

How did the Saxon Church affect the lives of Anglo-Saxons?
Religion played an important role in the lives of Anglo-Saxons.
- People were worried about what would happen when they died. The Church taught that sinful people were punished in the afterlife.
- They believed that God would punish sinful individuals or countries.

How did the Church affect the Anglo-Saxon king?
The king was seen as an agent of God, and his behaviour was expected to reflect this. For example, Edward the Confessor built Westminster Abbey.

EDWARD THE CONFESSOR
The life and reign of Edward the Confessor.

Who was Edward the Confessor?
Anglo-Saxon King Edward the Confessor ruled England from 1042 to 1066. When he died there was disagreement about who should succeed him to the throne.

How strong was Edward the Confessor?
Edward the Confessor generally managed to keep control, but problems developed during his reign.
- His earls and thegns were a powerful military force, and he relied on them to protect England from attack.
- He was a respected law-maker, who made decisions that kept the King's Peace and prevented in-fighting.
- He was very religious. Edward built Westminster Abbey, and reflected the Anglo-Saxon view of the king as an agent of God.
- However, he was not a warrior king, and did not win battles that allowed him to hand out land and money to his earls.
- Under Edward, Earl Godwin of Wessex and his family grew so strong that they had more military power than Edward.

What was Edward the Confessor's relationship with Normandy?
Although the Normans were a threat to England, Edward the Confessor had a strong relationship with them.
- His mother Emma, was a Norman.
- He went into exile in Normandy from 1016 to 1041, when the Vikings took over England.
- When he became king in 1042, Edward brought Norman advisers and supporters back to England with him.
- The Normans claimed that Edward promised the throne to William, duke of Normandy in return for his support against Earl Godwin.

What happened when Edward the Confessor died?
When Edward the Confessor died in January 1066, the Witan crowned Harold Godwinson as king.

Why did Edward the Confessor's death lead to a succession crisis?
Because Edward the Confessor died without an heir, it was not clear who should succeed him. The problem was that there was no definite way of choosing a successor.
- It helped to be a relative of the previous king, but it was not a guarantee.
- The Saxons thought that the previous king's dying words (novissima verba) were more important than any previous promises.
- However, the Normans considered that earlier promises were stronger, and could not be overturned.
- Ultimately, the Witan had to approve the next king, so it was possible for any potential king to influence their decision.

DID YOU KNOW?

Two facts about Edward the Confessor.
- He built Westminster Abbey in London, although it was rebuilt in the 13th century.
- He was made a saint, so he became Saint Edward the Confessor.

Get our free app at GCSEHistory.com

EARL GODWIN
The Godwin family - its power and relationship with Edward the Confessor.

Who was Earl Godwin?
Godwin was a powerful Anglo-Saxon *(p.17)* who was made Earl of Wessex in 1018 by King Cnut. Until his death in 1053 he built up the House of Godwin to become a powerful family. His power in England rivalled even that of Edward the Confessor.

Why was Earl Godwin so powerful?
There were a number of reasons why Godwin was able to become so powerful.
- ✅ King Edward allowed him to build *(p.75)* up his power, even though it meant that he could become a threat.
- ✅ He held extensive lands and was therefore very rich.
- ✅ He had a large family and a lot of sons, which meant that he had a lot of influential people protecting his interests.
- ✅ His family made good political marriages, which meant that he had family connections and ties of loyalty with Edward the Confessor, as well as with other earls and thegns.
- ✅ In 1045, Edward married Godwin's daughter, Edith, making Godwin the king's father-in-law.
- ✅ Edward was not a strong king, and relied on Godwin to help him keep control. This gave Godwin a lot of influence.

Why did Edward the Confessor allow Earl Godwin to build up his power?
There were a number of reasons why Edward the Confessor allowed Godwin to build *(p.75)* up so much power.
- ✅ He relied on Godwin's military support to help him keep control of England.
- ✅ He was married to Godwin's daughter, Edith, and family loyalty was important to the Anglo-Saxons.
- ✅ Godwin had helped Edward the Confessor to become king.
- ✅ Later, Edward the Confessor allowed the Godwin's family power to grow because he needed their help to protect England from the Norwegian threat, as well as from the Welsh.

What did Earl Godwin do?
Before his death in 1053, Godwin played an important role in the history of Anglo-Saxon England.
- ✅ He resisted the influence of Edward's Norman friends in England.
- ✅ He was exiled from England, but later returned.
- ✅ He put pressure on Edward the Confessor to agree to his plans.
- ✅ He built up the power of his family.

How was Godwin's relationship with the Normans?
He resisted the appointment of Normans to the nobility and the Church, and worked to get them sent home.

Why did Godwin go into exile?
In 1050, Godwin refused to punish the people of Dover after a deadly skirmish between visiting officials from Boulogne and townspeople. He was forced into exile as a result.

Why did Godwin return from exile?
In 1051, Godwin raised an army and pressured Edward into ending his exile and restoring his earldom.

How did Godwin increase the power of Godwin's family?
Godwin pressured Edward into giving important Church positions and earldoms to his sons and supporters.

Who were Godwin's rivals?
Few earls in England had the power to rival the Godwin family, but they were challenged by an alliance between Mercia and Wales.
- Aelfgar *(p.26)*, Earl of Mercia, was the only earl with the power to challenge Godwin.
- Aelfgar *(p.26)* worked with the Welsh king, Gruffudd ap Llywelyn.

How did the rivalry between Godwin and Aelfgar end?
After the death of Aelfgar *(p.26)*, Harold and Tostig Godwinson launched a joint attack on Gruffudd and defeated him.

What was the significance of the Godwin family?
By 1060, the Godwin family had become very powerful and controlled much of England. Before 1066 they were at the centre of some significant events in Anglo-Saxon England.
- In 1051, Godwin returned from exile.
- In 1062, after the death of Aelfgar *(p.26)*, the Godwinsons attacked Gruffudd, the Welsh king.
- In 1065, there was a rebellion *(p.47)* against Godwin's son, Tostig, in Northumbria.
- In 1064, Godwin's son Harold went on an official visit to Normandy.

Who was in the Godwin family?
One of the reasons for Godwin's power was his large family of sons. This gave him strong, loyal representatives in Anglo-Saxon England. Some of the most important members of the Godwin family were:
- Harold Godwinson.
- Tostig Godwinson.
- Gyrth Godwinson.
- Leofwine Godwinson.

Where did Godwin's son Harold rule?
Harold Godwinson became the Earl of Wessex after his father died.

Where did Godwin's son Tostig rule?
In 1055, Tostig Godwinson became the Earl of Northumbria, giving the Godwins a power base in the north of England.

Who did the Godwin family members marry?
The Godwin family made a series of politically helpful marriages that helped them to grow their power.
- Godwin's daughter, Edith, married Edward the Confessor.
- Harold married Edith the Fair, who owned large estates in East Anglia.
- Tostig married Judith, the daughter of the Count of Flanders.

EARL AELFGAR

Despite the Godwin family's power, it was not without its challenges - especially from Aelfgar, a rival earl.

Who was Earl Aelfgar?
In the 1050s and 1060s Aelfgar challenged the Godwin family by allying with the Welsh.

How did the Godwins respond to Aelfgar?
The Godwin family responded to the challenge from Aelfgar and Wales by eventually raising and leading armies to stop the threat.
- In the 1050s, Aelfgar was exiled twice, and returned to fight with the Welsh king, Gruffudd ap Llywelyn, against the Godwins.
- When Aelfgar died in 1062, the Godwins acted to stop the threat from Wales.
- They led a surprise attack on Gruffudd, although he managed to escape.
- Harold and Tostig then led their armies in a double attack, with Harold sailing around South Wales while Tostig marched into north Wales.
- Gruffudd was killed, and his head was sent to King Edward.
- Harold appointed a new puppet king in Wales, whom he could control.

REBELLION IN NORTHUMBRIA AGAINST TOSTIG

The career of Tostig Godwinson, leading to his death at the Battle of Stamford Bridge.

What was the revolt against Tostig?
In 1065, there was a revolt against Tostig Godwinson in Northumbria, where he had held the earldom since 1055.

Why was Northumbria important in the revolt against Tostig?
Northumbria was an important earldom for a number of reasons.
- It was very large.
- It bordered with Scotland, and therefore guarded England against attacks by the Scots.
- It was subject to attacks by the Vikings.
- It was a long way from the king's centre of power, and therefore was less easy to control.

Why was there a revolt against Tostig Godwinson in Northumbria in 1065?
There were a number of reasons for the revolt against Tostig.
- People in the Danelaw *(p.16)* had different customs and language *(p.77)*, while Tostig was a southerner. There may have been misunderstandings and resentment based on that.
- Tostig taxed the area more heavily than the people were used to.
- Tostig was friendly with the Scottish king, Malcolm III, and therefore didn't defend the area from, or retaliate after Scottish attacks.
- Northumbrians claimed that he had falsely accused them of crimes so that he could confiscate their land and money to use against his rivals.
- Tostig ordered the assassination of his Northumbrian rivals.

What happened in the Northumbrian revolt against Tostig?
The revolt against Tostig in Northumbria occurred in October 1065.
- At the beginning of October, important Northumbrian earls marched on York, killing Tostig's supporters and declaring him an outlaw.
- Morcar, the brother of Edwin, the Earl of Mercia, was invited to be Earl of Northumbria by the rebels.
- Instead of marching on the north, Harold Godwinson met with the rebels and agreed to their terms. He also married Edwin and Morcar's sister.
- Tostig was exiled on 1st November 1065.

What were the results of the Tostig revolt?
The Northumbrian revolt (p.47) had a number of results.
- King Edward raised an army to put down the revolt (p.47), but it wasn't used.
- Harold and the earls successfully negotiated with Edward to prevent the army marching on Northumbria, showing the limits of the power of the king.
- Tostig was exiled, and was furious with Harold, accusing him of a plot to overthrow him.
- Morcar became Earl of Northumbria. The Northumbrians chose him as their ruler, even though he was a southerner like Tostig.

THE SUCCESSION CRISIS
The contenders for the English throne after the death of Edward the Confessor.

What was the succession crisis of 1066?
After Edward the Confessor died on 5th January, 1066, there was a struggle for the throne of England between four men. The crisis ended with the Battle of Hastings (p.38) on 14th October, 1066.

Why were there different contenders for the throne after Edward the Confessor died?
Because Edward the Confessor was childless when he died, it wasn't clear who should succeed him as king. Several people claimed to be his rightful heir.

Which contenders had claims on the throne of England after Edward the Confessor's death?
Four people had claims to the throne of England.
- Harold Godwinson.
- Edgar Aetheling.
- Harald Hardrada, who was supported by Tostig Godwinson.
- William, duke of Normandy.

Which contender to the throne in 1066 had the strongest claim?
The contenders for the throne in 1066 all claimed the throne through family relationships. These were either blood relationships, or through marriage or other agreements.
- Edgar Aetheling was Edward the Confessor's closest blood relative - his great-nephew. He was called the Aetheling, which was a name that indicated an heir apparent.
- Harold Godwinson was Edward the Confessor's brother-in-law. His sister, Edith, was married to Edward.

- William, Duke of Normandy, was related to Edward the Confessor through his great-aunt, Emma of Normandy, who was Edward's mother.
- Harald Hardrada inherited the claim to the throne through an agreement between Harthacnut and Magnus, which Harald claimed extended to him.

Which contender to the throne in 1066 one had the strongest army?

The contenders for the throne in 1066 were supported by varying degrees of military power.

- Harold Godwinson had the support of the Witan, thegns and earls in England. This meant that he could raise an army of about 8,000 men, with potentially many more from the fyrd.
- William had years of military experience. He had a strong, skilled army of at least 7,000 men, including archers and cavalry.
- Harald Hardrada had a strong fleet of about 300 ships, and could raise as many as 10,000 soldiers.
- Edgar was fifteen when Edward died. He had no military experience, and no wealth. That meant he had little military support to defend the kingdom.

Which contender to the throne did Edward the Confessor choose?

Edward the Confessor's choice of successor after his death was a point of disagreement between the contenders.

- William, duke of Normandy claimed to have an agreement with Edward the Confessor, made in 1051, that he would inherit the throne if Edward died childless.
- The Anglo-Saxons claimed that, on his deathbed, Edward promised the crown to Harold Godwinson.
- Edgar's name 'Aetheling' was an Anglo-Saxon word meaning 'heir', but as he was a child when Edward died, it was unlikely that Edward saw him as the next king.
- Harald Hardrada's claim bypassed Edward completely, and instead originated from King Harthacnut.

What alliances did the contenders to the throne have in 1066?

The contenders to the throne had important alliances in 1066.

- Harold Godwinson had the support of thegns, earls and Witan in England. They wanted a strong military leader, and so preferred his claim to Edgar Aetheling's.
- William had the support of the pope. He also claimed that Harold Godwinson had sworn to support his claim during his Normandy embassy of 1064.
- Harald Hardrada had the support of Tostig Godwinson, Harold's brother. There was also a possibility that he might be a popular choice in the Danelaw (p. 16).

What nationality were the contenders to the throne in 1066?

Many of the Saxons disliked the idea of a foreign king. They had objected to the number of Normans that Edward had invited to England in the 1050s.

- Harold Godwinson and Edgar Aetheling were English.
- William, Duke of Normandy, was a Norman from a region of France.
- Harald Hardrada was the King of Norway.

HAROLD GODWINSON

The life and career of Harold Godwinson, his claim to the throne, and his death at the Battle of Hastings.

Who was Harold Godwinson?
Harold Godwinson was the Earl of Wessex and the most powerful noble in England at the death of Edward the Confessor. He became King Harold II of England but lost the Battle of Hastings *(p.38)* to William, Duke of Normandy.

Who was Harold Godwinson's family?
Harold was part of the powerful Anglo-Saxon *(p.17)* Godwin family.
- His father, Godwin, was a thegn who was made Earl of Wessex by King Cnut and grew very powerful.
- His brothers, including Tostig, Leofwine and Gyrth, were also powerful Anglo-Saxon *(p.17)* earls.
- His wife, Edith the Fair, owned large amounts of land in East Anglia.

Where was Harold Godwinson based?
Harold was Earl of Wessex, a large area of land in the south of England.

How did Harold Godwinson get on with his brother?
Harold's relationship with his brother, Tostig, deteriorated in the 1060s.
- In 1062, they led a joint attack on the Welsh king, Gruffydd ap Llywelyn.
- In 1065, Harold refused to support Tostig when Northumbria rebelled against him.
- Tostig was exiled and plotted with Harald Hardrada to overthrow Harold.

Why did Harold Godwinson support the Northumbrian rebels against his brother?
Historians aren't sure why Harold Godwinson acted against his own brother, Tostig, in the Northumbrian revolt *(p.47)*, but there are some suggestions:
- He agreed with other earls that Tostig was to blame for running Northumbria badly.
- Edward was old, and Harold was more focused on becoming king than on promoting his family's interests.
- Tostig was a possible rival for the throne if Edward died.
- Harold needed a united kingdom to fight off the threats from Denmark and Normandy.

What was Harold Godwinson's Norman Embassy?
In 1064, Harold travelled to Normandy, in an embassy on behalf of King Edward. It was a significant visit.

Why did Harold Godwinson go to Normandy?
Harold Godwinson travelled to see William, Duke of Normandy, in 1064 on a mission for King Edward. However, the exact reason for his visit is unclear.
- The Normans claimed that King Edward asked Harold to talk to William about succeeding him as king, and that Harold swore allegiance to William.
- The Anglo-Saxons claimed that Harold went to negotiate the release of his brother and nephew (Wulfnoth and Hakon), who were William's hostages.

What happened on Harold Godwinson's journey to Normandy?
Harold's journey to Normandy was eventful.
- He travelled to France, but was blown off course and landed at Ponthieu.

- He was taken prisoner by Count Guy of Ponthieu.
- William demanded that Count Guy hand Harold over to him.

What did Harold Godwinson do in Normandy?

Whilst in Normandy, Harold and William worked together fairly successfully. Harold performed a number of tasks for William.
- He stayed with William.
- He delivered Edward's message to William.
- He fought with William in two military campaigns.
- He received gifts of armour and weapons as a sign of William's gratitude.
- The Normans claimed that, by the end of the visit, Harold was prepared to take an oath of allegiance to William.

Did Harold Godwinson swear an oath to William?

While in Normandy, Harold made an oath to William, on two holy relics.
- The Normans claimed that this was an oath of allegiance, with Harold promising to support William's claim to the throne.
- However, while Harold did not dispute that he took an oath, he did not agree that he supported William's claim to the throne.

What was the significance of Harold Godwinson's visit to Normandy?

Harold's visit to William, and his oath, were significant for a number of reasons.
- It demonstrated how much Edward the Confessor trusted and relied on Harold.
- It showed how close England and Normandy were, which boosted William's claim to the throne.
- It allowed the Normans to claim that Harold was an oath-breaker when he took the throne after Edward's death.

Why did Harold Godwinson think he should be king?

Harold Godwinson, Earl of Wessex, had several reasons for claiming the throne when Edward the Confessor died in 1066.
- He was Edward's brother-in-law.
- He had great military power and a history of military success.
- He had influence and support among the earls and thegns.
- He had been the king's trusted advisor and right-hand man. He had even acted as 'sub regulus' (deputy king) for Edward.
- He claimed that Edward, on his deathbed, had nominated him to be king.

What were the strengths of Harold Godwinson's claim to the throne?

Harold Godwinson was one of the strongest claimants to the crown of England in 1066.
- He had the support of thegns, earls and the Witan in England. This gave him considerable support from the military power of England.
- He had been nominated as Edward's successor by the king himself, on his deathbed, and had witnesses to support his claim.

What were the weaknesses of Harold Godwinson's claim to the throne?

There were reasons why Harold's claim to the throne was opposed.
- William, duke of Normandy challenged his claim that Edward had wanted Harold as king.
- Harold wasn't related to the king by blood.

When did Harold Godwinson take power?
On 6th January 1066 - the day of Edward's burial - Harold Godwinson was crowned Harold II of England.

Why was Harold Godwinson made king in 1066?
Harold was, essentially, in the right place at the right time.
- He moved fast and seized his opportunity.
- The Witan agreed that he should be king.

Why did the Witan choose Harold Godwinson?
The Witan agreed that Harold Godwinson should become king on the 5th January 1066, the day of Edward's death. There were a number of reasons for this.
- They were already gathered for the opening of Westminster Abbey in London.
- They were aware of the threat from Normandy, and wanted a warrior king who could take swift action.
- They were likely to object to a Norman king - as Godwin had objected to Edward's Norman advisers.

What challenges did Harold Godwinson face as king?
As soon as he became king, Harold faced threats and challenges.
- Other English earls might not agree with the choice, particularly those from Mercia, which was Wessex's rival.
- Northumbria might not accept Tostig's brother as king.
- Tostig was in Europe, bitter and angry at Harold and looking for allies.
- William of Normandy was reported to be building (p.75) an invasion fleet.

What did Harold Godwinson do after his coronation?
Immediately after his coronation, Harold took swift action to deal with the threats to his rule.
- He travelled to York, to ensure that he had the support of Northumbrian members of the Witan, who had not been in London. This was to ensure that the north would remain loyal.
- To strengthen his position, he married the sister of the earls Edwin and Morcar.
- He gathered a large army and fleet from the fyrd, and positioned them on the south coast of England to guard against an invasion from Normandy.
- He kept the army in one place all summer, until the autumn when it was time for them to stand down and return home.

How did Tostig react when Harold Godwinson was crowned?
Since his exile, Harold's brother Tostig had been gathering support and plotting revenge.
- He gained support in Flanders, where his wife was from, and sailed a fleet to England in May 1066.
- When he found out about the strength of Harold's army, Tostig diverted his path to Lincolnshire.
- In Lincolnshire, a fight with the Mercians destroyed most of his fleet.
- Tostig fled to Scotland and began to plot with Harald Hardrada.

Which battles did Harold Godwinson fight in 1066?
In 1066, Harold Godwinson led his army into 2 significant battles:
- The Battle of Stamford Bridge (p.36) on 25th September, in which Harald Hardrada and Tostig Godwinson were defeated and killed.
- The Battle of Hastings (p.38) on 14th October, in which he was defeated and killed by the Norman army of William, Duke of Normandy.

What did Harold Godwinson do once he was king in 1066?
Once he was king, Harold took decisive action to defend England from threats.
- ✅ He assembled his army on the south coast to wait for a Norman attack.
- ✅ He responded to news of a Viking attack by taking his army north to defeat Harald Hardrada at Stamford Bridge.
- ✅ He returned with his troops to London on hearing news of William's attack on the south.
- ✅ He led his troops out to meet the Norman army at Hastings.
- ✅ He fought and lost against William's Norman army at the Battle of Hastings *(p.41)* on 14th October 1066.

What were Harold Godwinson's tactics in the Battle of Hastings?
At the Battle of Hastings *(p.38)*, the Anglo-Saxons' main tactic was to capture the high ground, and use the shield wall to form an impenetrable defensive position. This tactic depended on the shield wall holding in the face of attack.

What advantages did Harold Godwinson have at Hastings?
Harold and the Anglo-Saxon army *(p.19)* had some advantages at the Battle of Hastings *(p.38)*. Two of the most important were:
- ✅ Holding the high ground at the top of Senlac Hill.
- ✅ The shield wall.

Did poor discipline lead to Harold Godwinson's defeat?
There was poor discipline in Harold's army which led to a weakening of the shield wall. Harold's foot soldiers, the fyrd, broke ranks to chase retreating Normans. This allowed the Norman cavalry to encircle them and cut them down.

Did Harold Godwinson's poor timing lead to his defeat?
Some historians believe that Harold summoned the fyrd too early. The long wait over the summer meant he was forced to disband the army before the Normans arrived.

Was Harold Godwinson's lack of readiness a reason for his defeat?
Harold marched out to meet the Normans before the fyrd had completely reassembled. Norman intelligence was better than the Anglo-Saxons', and they weren't ready when the Normans attacked on the morning of 14th October.

Did Harold Godwinson leave his army exposed out of London?
Harold also decided to meet William in the English countryside, instead of remaining within well-defended London and letting the Normans besiege it. This is seen as a mistake, although there were arguments for and against the strategy.

Why should Harold Godwinson have waited in London instead of going to Hastings?
Harold waited in London for 5 days, to allow his troops to arrive before marching on Hastings. It can be argued the decision to leave London was a mistake.
- ✅ It would have been more difficult for William to besiege London than to fight a battle in open countryside.
- ✅ Harold could have waited for the full levy of the fyrd to arrive.
- ✅ Harold would have been unable to surprise William anyway, because of the intelligence William received from his spies.
- ✅ Harold may have shown poor judgement by rushing into battle because he was angry at reports of Norman brutality in the English countryside.

Why was it better for Harold Godwinson to leave London?

There are a number of reasons why it leaving London to meet the Normans at Hastings was the best decision Harold could have made.

- ✅ Wessex was Harold's home, and it was his responsibility to protect his people from Norman brutality.
- ✅ It was possible for the Anglo-Saxons to gain the element of surprise over the Normans, or to trap them at Hastings.
- ✅ William and the Normans were skilled and experienced in sieges. On the other hand, the Anglo-Saxons had little knowledge of defending a city.
- ✅ Edwin and Morcar may have refused to help Harold against William, and therefore leaving London made less of a difference to Harold's available forces.

How did Harold Godwinson die?

Harold was killed at Hastings, possibly by an arrow in the eye. This was a random event that had a huge impact on the outcome of the battle.

HARALD HARDRADA

Harald Hardrada, the Norwegian king who claimed the English throne and was killed at the Battle of Stamford Bridge.

Who was Harald Hardrada?

Harald Hardrada was the King of Norway. In 1066 he invaded England in an attempt to take the throne.

Why did Harald Hardrada think he should be king?

There were a number of reasons why Harald Hardrada had a claim to the throne.

- ✅ His predecessor in Norway, Magnus, had made an agreement with Harthacnut, a previous Viking king of England.
- ✅ The agreement said that, if Harthacnut died before Magnus, then Magnus would succeed him as king of England.
- ✅ This had not happened, but as Magnus' successor in Norway, Harald believed that the agreement extended to him.

What were the strengths of Harald Hardrada's claim to the throne?

Harald Hardrada felt his claim was strong.

- ✅ He had succeeded to the Norwegian throne when Magnus died, so he felt that Magnus' agreement with Harthacnut extended to him.
- ✅ England had been ruled by Vikings from 1016 to 1042. Many Anglo-Danes lived in England, and might welcome another Viking king.

What were the weaknesses of Harald Hardrada's claim to the throne?

Harald Hardrada's claim was not, in fact, particularly strong.

- ✅ The agreement between Magnus and Harthacnut had been between the two kings, and it did not extend to their successors.
- ✅ Although many Anglo-Danes might have accepted Harald, most people in England did not want a Viking king.
- ✅ Harald had no other ties or relationship with England.
- ✅ There is no evidence that Harald intended to claim the throne until he was urged to do so by Tostig Godwinson in 1066.

How strong was Harald Hardrada?
In 1066, Harald was able to muster a fleet of 300 ships and up to 10,000 soldiers.

Who were Harald Hardrada's allies?
Harald Hardrada allied with Tostig Godwinson, Harold's brother.

What did Harald Hardrada do?
In September 1066 Harald Hardrada led a Viking invasion *(p.37)* on the north-east of England.

Which battles did Harald Hardrada fight in England?
During the Viking attack on England, Harald Hardrada was involved in two important battles:
- ✅ The Battle of Gate Fulford *(p.36)*, in which he defeated the army of Anglo-Saxon earls Edwin and Morcar.
- ✅ The Battle of Stamford Bridge *(p.36)*, against Harold Godwinson and his Anglo-Saxon army *(p.19)*. Hardrada was defeated and killed in this battle.

DID YOU KNOW?

Two facts about Harald Hardrada:
- ✓ Hardrada means 'hard ruler'.
- ✓ In his younger days, Hardrada served in the Varangian Guard in Constantinople. His boss was the Eastern Roman emperor.

EDGAR AETHELING
Edgar Aetheling, the royal prince who lost his bid to become King of England.

Who was Edgar Aetheling?
Edgar Aetheling was the great-nephew of Edward the Confessor. As Edward's closest male relative, he was a contender for the throne in 1066, and was later involved in rebellions against the Normans.

Why did Edgar Aetheling think he should be king?
Edgar Aetheling was Edward the Confessor's closest male relative, so he thought he had a good claim to the throne.

What were the strengths of Edgar Aetheling's claim to the throne?
Edgar Aetheling appeared to have a strong claim to the English throne.
- ✅ He was Edward the Confessor's closest blood relative - his great-nephew.
- ✅ His father, Edward the Exile, had been nominated to succeed Edward the Confessor, but had died before Edward. However, as the Exile's son, Edgar felt he should take his father's place.
- ✅ Edgar had been brought up by Edward the Confessor. He was called the Aetheling, which was a name that indicated an heir apparent.

What were the weaknesses of Edgar Aetheling's claim to the throne?
Edgar Aetheling's claim was not considered strong for a number of reasons.

- He was only around fifteen when Edward the Confessor died. The Witan thought he was too young to lead England when there were other stronger claimants who might invade.
- Edgar had no military experience, and no wealth. That meant he had little military support to defend the kingdom.
- There was no law that said that the throne should go to the previous king's closest male relative.
- Because he had been born in Hungary and had lived there for the first few years of his life, Edgar was not well known to the nobles.

When was Edgar Aetheling crowned king?

Following Harold Godwinson's defeat at Hastings in October 1066, Edgar was hastily crowned king in London. However, he and other important Anglo-Saxon earls surrendered to William, Duke of Normandy shortly afterwards, at Berkhamsted.

What rebellions was Edgar Aetheling involved in?

Edgar Aetheling was involved in a number of uprisings following the Norman conquest.
- He was involved in Edwin and Morcar's rebellion *(p.47)* of 1068.
- He led a rebellion *(p.47)* of Anglo-Saxons and Danish invaders in 1069.

VIKING INVASION, 1066

Harald Hardrada's invasion of England in 1066.

What was the Viking invasion in 1066?

In September 1066, Tostig and Hardrada launched an invasion on England.

What did the invading Vikings do first in 1066?

The Viking attack came as a surprise to the English.
- Hardrada had about 300 ships in his fleet, and perhaps 10,000 Viking soldiers.
- They landed at the River Humber and marched up to York.
- At Gate Fulford *(p.36)*, outside York, they met an army led by Morcar, Earl of Northumbria and his brother Edwin, Earl of Mercia, who decided to meet the invaders outside the city.

What happened in the Viking invasion of England in 1066.

The Viking invasion *(p.37)* of 1066 involved two main battles.
- The Battle of Gate Fulford *(p.36)* against the brothers Edwin and Morcar, Earls of Mercia and Northumbria, was a resounding defeat for the Anglo-Saxons.
- The Battle of Stamford Bridge *(p.36)*, against King Harold and his army, led to defeat for the Vikings.

BATTLE OF GATE FULFORD, 1066

The Battle of Gate Fulford, where Harald Hardrada defeated the Saxons.

What happened at the Battle of Gate Fulford?

The Battle of Gate Fulford was a crushing defeat for the Anglo-Saxons, who were led by Earls Edwin and Morcar.

Why did the Anglo-Saxons lose the battle of Gate Fulford?

There were a number of reasons why Edwin and Morcar were disadvantaged in the Battle of Gate Fulford.
- They might have been outnumbered. Although many Vikings stayed with the ships, Hardrada and Tostig's forces numbered up to 10,000. Edwin and Morcar are believed to have had 6,000 men.
- Harald Hardrada was a good tactician and an experienced warrior.
- Edwin and Morcar stationed their troops in front of marshland, leaving them nowhere to retreat.

What were the events of the Battle of Gate Fulford?

Hardrada positioned Tostig's weaker troops at one wing of his army.
- When the Anglo-Saxons charged them, Hardrada brought his stronger soldiers to attack them from the side.
- The English army broke and tried to retreat, but ran into the marsh and got stuck.
- The Vikings cut the Anglo-Saxons down, and claimed that they could avoid getting their boots muddy in the marsh by walking on the English corpses.
- Edwin and Morcar escaped from the slaughter, but it is very likely they were too weakened to play any role in the later battles of Stamford Bridge and Hastings.

How did Harold Godwinson react to the Viking invasion at the Battle of Gate Fulford?

When Harold learned of the Viking invasion *(p.37)* he brought his housecarls north to meet them.
- Harold learnt of the Viking invasion *(p.37)*, possibly through beacon signals, but did not know about the Battle of Gate Fulford.
- The southern fyrd, which had been disbanded on the 8th September, was recalled.

What did Harold's journey to the north involve in 1066 for the Battle of Gate Fulford?

Harold's army had a long journey in order to meet the Viking invaders in the north.
- On 20th September, Harold set off, leading his housecarls on the 185-mile journey north.
- He sent messages to gather a new army to travel ahead of him, gathering troops from East Anglia and Mercia.
- It isn't clear how Harold travelled north. It may have been on foot, but it is possible his army sailed up the coast.

BATTLE OF STAMFORD BRIDGE, 1066

The Battle of Stamford Bridge, where Harold Godwinson defeated Harald Hardrada's army and saved England from the Viking invasion.

What was the Battle of Stamford Bridge?

The Battle of Stamford Bridge was fought on 25th September, 1066, between Hardrada and Tostig's Viking invaders, and Harold Godwinson's Anglo-Saxon army *(p.19)*.

What happened at the Battle of Stamford Bridge?

The Battle of Stamford Bridge was a victory for Harold's Anglo-Saxon army *(p.19)*.

- Hardrada and Tostig had demanded hostages from all over Yorkshire, and were waiting for them at Stamford Bridge.
- Harold and his army launched a surprise attack on the Vikings from behind a small hill overlooking Stamford Bridge.
- Hardrada and Tostig were both killed, and it was reported that only 24 Viking ships (out of the original 300) returned home.

Why did Harold win the Battle of Stamford Bridge?

Harold had several military advantages at the Battle of Stamford Bridge.

- The Vikings had left their armour on their ships as it was a hot day, along with around a third of their men.
- Harold took Hardrada and Tostig completely by surprise, as they had not expected him to arrive in the north so quickly.
- Hardrada's army had recently fought a battle, and were not expecting another so soon.
- Harold's housecarls showed endurance and skill in breaking the Viking shield wall.

> **DID YOU KNOW?**
>
> **The Battle of Stamford Bridge has a connection with Chelsea Football Club.**
>
> The club's stadium - Stamford Bridge - was named after a bridge next to the ground originally called 'Samfordesbrigge' - literally, the 'bridge at the sandy ford'.

SIGNIFICANCE OF THE VIKING INVASION

The significance of the English victory at Stamford Bridge and its implications for England.

What was the significance of the Viking invasion of England?

The Viking defeat helped the Norman invasion to succeed.

How did the Viking invasion help the Normans?

The Viking invasion meant that Harold's army wasn't waiting on the south coast when the Normans landed in late September 1066. Unfortunately, the fyrd had already been disbanded before Harold's army marched north.

Did the Viking invasion make much difference to Harold's army at Hastings?

Although Harold had been victorious, he had lost men at both Gate Fulford *(p.36)* and Stamford Bridge. These included the professional housecarls. As a result, he could call on fewer experienced warriors to fight against William's Norman army.

Did Edwin and Morcar fight at the Battle of Hastings after losing against the Vikings invasion?

Edwin and Morcar do not appear in the records of the Battle of Hastings *(p.38)*. It could be that they refused - or were not in a position - to fight after their defeat, but it could also be that they just weren't mentioned.

How tired were Harold's troops after defeating the Viking invasion?
Harold's recent battle and march south must have exhausted his housecarls. However, after their great victory, morale would have been high.

Did the defeat of the Viking army make Harold overconfident?
Harold may have chosen to meet William outside London because he was over-confident after his victory over Hardrada. However, the Anglo-Saxons had been expecting the Normans for a long time.

THE NORMAN THREAT
The extent of William of Normandy's threat to England and Harold's efforts to contain it.

What was the Norman threat to England in 1066?
Since Harold's coronation, reports had informed him that William, Duke of Normandy was preparing an invasion fleet. Harold had stationed an army and a fleet on the south coast, but by September this had been disbanded.

Why did Harold leave England unprotected against the Norman threat in 1066?
Events showed that abandoning the south coast to face the Vikings was not a good decision for Harold to make. However, he had a number of reasons for doing so.
- ☑ The fyrd needed to return home and look after their farms and families, and to gather the harvest.
- ☑ The Viking invasion *(p.37)* presented a more immediate threat.
- ☑ The September storms had wrecked some of Harold's ships, and had probably affected William's in the same way.
- ☑ There was a strong northerly wind that prevented the Normans from sailing when originally planned.
- ☑ It was difficult to keep a standing army for a long time, and Harold knew that William must have faced the same difficulties that he had.

How did Harold respond to the Norman threat in 1066?
Harold faced the Norman threat by gathering a huge army and fleet from the fyrd on the south coast. However, in September this was disbanded, and Harold marched north to deal with the Vikings.

When was the Norman threat finally realised in 1066?
On 1st October, 1066, less than a week after the Battle of Stamford Bridge *(p.36)*, King Harold received word that William and the Norman army had landed on the south coast on 28th September.

BATTLE OF HASTINGS, 1066
The Battle of Hastings, which was on 14th October, 1066.

What was the Battle of Hastings?
The Battle of Hastings took place between the armies of William, Duke of Normandy and Harold Godwinson, king of England. It was a victory for the Normans.

When was the Battle of Hastings?
The Battle of Hastings took place on 14th October, 1066.

 What happened at the Battle of Hastings?
The exact events of the Battle of Hastings are unclear, but some things are known.
- William was aware of Harold's approach and there was a dash for the top of the hill, which the Anglo-Saxons won. Gaining the higher ground gave the Anglo-Saxons an advantage.
- The Anglo-Saxons formed a shield wall at the top of the hill, which the Norman archers could not break. William sent his foot soldiers up the hill, followed by his cavalry, but they could not break the wall.
- At one point, a rumour went round the Norman troops that William had been killed. He lifted his helmet to show his face and rally them.
- Harold's shield wall was weakened when some Anglo-Saxons broke ranks to chase the retreating Normans. The Normans continued to reduce the shield wall until the remainder was broken.

 How did the Battle of Hastings end?
With the shield wall broken, the Norman cavalry charged the Anglo-Saxons. Harold Godwinson, his brothers Gyrth and Leofwine and most of their housecarls were killed. The remaining troops fled.

 What armies did Harold Godwinson and William have at the Battle of Hastings?
The fact that the Battle of Hastings lasted all day suggests that the two armies were fairly evenly matched. Both had a core of well-trained, well-equipped men, alongside ordinary soldiers.
- William is thought to have had about 4,000-6,000 troops, with about 800 elite knights. His army included cavalry and archers.
- Harold led about 6,000-7,000 soldiers, some of whom were housecarls.

 How did the Anglo-Saxons use the shield wall at the Battle of Hastings?
The shield wall at the top of the hill protected the Anglo-Saxon army *(p.19)* against arrows and the Norman cavalry. While it remained disciplined, it was very difficult to break.
- It involved setting troops out in several close-set, parallel lines. The men at the front overlapped their shields and stuck their spears through the gaps.
- The shield wall formed a strong defensive position, effective against archers and difficult even for cavalry to break.
- It relied on discipline of the troops to hold the line.
- It was an effective tactic that had been used by Harald Hardrada at the Battle of Gate Fulford *(p.36)*.

 What were the advantages of the higher ground in the Battle of Hastings?
Holding the higher ground was an advantage for the Anglo-Saxons. The Norman cavalry could not charge uphill at the strength needed to break the shield wall, and archers struggled to shoot up at Harold's troops.

 How did the different sorts of soldiers help William in the Battle of Hastings?
The Norman troops had a variety of skills and tactics, while the Anglo-Saxons tended to fight in a similar way every time. This meant that William could try different methods of attack until he found one that worked.

 How did the cavalry help the Norman army win the Battle of Hastings?
The Norman cavalry was a deadly force, with a strong charge and a height advantage in combat. Once the shield wall was broken, they devastated the Anglo-Saxon troops.

Why were the archers an advantage in the Battle of Hastings?
Once the shield wall was broken and the Norman archers could get closer to the Anglo-Saxon troops, they were able to cause great damage from a distance. Harold may have been killed by an arrow to the eye.

Did discipline make a difference in the Battle of Hastings?
The discipline of the Norman troops meant that they continued to form co-ordinated attacks using a variety of tactics, while the lack of discipline in the Anglo-Saxon army *(p. 19)* led to the breaking of the shield wall.

What was the feigned retreat tactic that William used at the Battle of Hastings?
During the battle the Normans feigned (faked) a retreat, causing the fyrd to break the shield wall and run down the hill to give chase. William's cavalry then doubled back and cut them down. This happened three times.

How did experimenting with battle tactics help William in the Battle of Hastings?
After his cavalry and archers' attacks on the Saxon position failed, William was able to use the feigned retreat to weaken the shield wall. Once it was weakened, he then deployed his archers and cavalry to break it completely.

What were the reasons for Harold Godwinson's defeat in the Battle of Hastings?
Although the Battle of Hastings was strongly influenced by luck and chance, some of Harold's decisions and tactics showed weakness. These included:
- ✅ Poor discipline of his troops.
- ✅ Poor timing of his defences.
- ✅ His unreadiness for the battle.
- ✅ His decision to leave London and meet William at Hastings.

How important was luck at the Battle of Hastings?
Although both the Anglo-Saxons and Normans had their strengths and weaknesses, the outcome of Hastings was also influenced by luck and chance. This was seen as 'God's will' by people at the time.
- ✅ Harold was killed at Hastings, possibly by an arrow in the eye. This was a random event that gave William victory.
- ✅ Harold was unlucky that the Vikings attacked shortly before the Normans sailed. Even though Harold had already disbanded the fyrd, this put the Anglo-Saxon troops at a disadvantage and meant they were exhausted by the time they arrived at Hastings.
- ✅ The weather was bad enough to damage the English fleet and to convince Harold that William wouldn't strike, but not bad enough to stop the Normans from sailing to England.

DID YOU KNOW?

Three facts about the Battle of Hastings:
- ✔ It took place near the modern town of Battle, around 7 miles from Hastings; the town was named after the event.
- ✔ There is some disagreement about exactly where the battle took place. The traditional site was known as Senlac Hill, but a recent theory claims it was fought at nearby Caldbec Hill.
- ✔ In the 1070s, a huge embroidery - known as the Bayeux Tapestry - was created to show the events of the battle. It is 68 metres long!

ARMIES AND TACTICS AT THE BATTLE OF HASTINGS
The Norman and Saxon armies at Hastings, and the tactics used by William and Harold.

 How was the Battle of Hastings fought by the armies?
The two sides in the Battle of Hastings (p.38) fought with different tactics and in different styles.

 What was the Norman army like at the Battle of Hastings?
William's army consisted of knights on horseback, archers, and infantry (footmen).

 What were the Norman archers like in the Battle of Hastings?
Norman archers had padded jackets, called gambesons, as armour. They included crossbowmen.

 What were the Norman knights like in the Battle of Hastings?
Knights were William's elite troops. They were skilled, well-equipped, and fought on horseback.
- ☑ Their weapons included lances, javelins, swords and maces.
- ☑ War-horses were called destriers. They were especially bred to be strong enough to carry an armoured knight (p.67), and trained to be vicious in battle.
- ☑ Their shields were kite-shaped to protect the left side.
- ☑ Their armour was chain mail, and they wore a conical helmet with a nose-piece.
- ☑ Saddles held the knights in place to free their arms for fighting, while stirrups allowed them to stand up for extra power in attacks. Spurs were used to direct their horses in manoeuvres.
- ☑ Knights carried a gonfanon, a flag to signal manoeuvres.
- ☑ Knights spent years training to fight effectively on horseback.

 What was the Norman infantry like at the Battle of Hastings?
The infantry, or foot-soldiers, of the Norman army probably had chain mail, shields, swords and javelins.

 What was the Anglo-Saxon army like at the Battle of Hastings?
It is not known how many housecarls Harold brought to the Battle of Hastings (p.38), but the Anglo-Saxon army (p.19) had a well-trained, well-equipped core, along with the men of the fyrd.

 What were the Anglo-Saxon housecarls like at the Battle of Hastings?
The housecarls were the elite of the Anglo-Saxon army (p.19). They were formidable soldiers who fought on foot.
- ☑ They were armed with swords, javelins, and long heavy axes.
- ☑ They carried a round wooden shield, with a metal boss in the centre for reinforcement.
- ☑ Housecarls were trained to open gaps in the shield wall for axe blows, then to close it up again. They were skilled with their axes and had great strength, discipline, and endurance.
- ☑ Their armour was chain mail, or metal plates sewn onto leather. They also had a conical helmet with a nose-piece.

 Who were the Anglo-Saxon fyrd at the Battle of Hastings?
Harold had had to call the fyrd quickly as he marched back south, and some had not turned up on time, possibly including his own archers. The thegns had proper weapons, but many of the fyrd were armed only with farm tools.

Why did the Anglo-Saxon army not have horses at the Battle of Hastings?

The Norman cavalry turned out to be an advantage in the Battle of Hastings (p.38), but there were a number of reasons why the Anglo-Saxons did not fight on horseback.

- ☑ Instead of horses, the Anglo-Saxons invested in their fleet, and in fortifying towns against attacks from the sea. This was based on long experience of dealing with Viking invasions.
- ☑ The Norman cavalry was the result of years of breeding horses, training knights, and developing technology such as the saddle and lance. Developing good cavalry was difficult, expensive and time-consuming.

THE ENGLISH SURRENDER OF 1066
The aftermath of the Battle of Hastings, and the surrender of the Saxon lords.

What was the surrender of the English after the Battle of Hastings?
Within a few weeks of Harold Godwinson's defeat at the Battle of Hastings (p.38), the other earls of England had surrendered to William's rule. However, at first it seemed as though they might continue to fight.

What happened in the surrender of the Anglo-Saxons after the Battle of Hastings?
After the Battle of Hastings (p.38), the Anglo-Saxons in London looked as though they might continue the fight.

- ☑ Surviving troops from Hastings fled to London, where they met with the reinforcements from the fyrd, who had not arrived at Hastings in time.
- ☑ The Witan elected Edgar Aetheling as king. The Archbishops Stigand of Canterbury and Ealdred of York crowned him, and he was also supported by Edwin and Morcar.
- ☑ Edwin and Morcar sent their sister and Harold's widow, Ealdgyth, to Chester for safety.

How did William cause the English surrender after the Battle of Hastings?
William had a number of priorities following his victory at the Battle of Hastings (p.38).

- ☑ He secured the south coast, so that supplies and more troops could be sent from Normandy, although he and many of his army became ill at Dover.
- ☑ He sent soldiers to seize the royal treasury at Winchester.
- ☑ He then headed to London to force a surrender, destroying people's homes as he went.
- ☑ Instead of directly approaching heavily-fortified London, he first went north-west to Berkhamsted.

Who surrendered to William in 1066 after the Battle of Hastings?
At Berkhamsted, Edgar Aetheling met William, along with Archbishop Ealdred, Edwin, Morcar, and other leading earls. They surrendered to William, swore oaths to obey him, gave him hostages, and offered him the crown.

Why did the Anglo-Saxons surrender after the Battle of Hastings?
It isn't clear why the Anglo-Saxons surrendered to William in 1066, as they were in a good position to continue fighting. However, the earls clearly felt that submission was the better option, perhaps because William had some key strengths.

How were the Anglo-Saxons in a good position to avoid surrender after the Battle of Hastings?
The Anglo-Saxons had several strengths against the Normans after the Battle of Hastings (p.38).

- ☑ London was well-fortified and a siege would cause losses and problems for William.

- William was in a foreign country, with only the soldiers he had brought with him. By contrast, the Saxons could potentially gather a new army to oppose him.
- Although William might have gained Wessex, Edwin and Morcar's earldoms of Mercia and Northumbria were large and important parts of England.

What Anglo-Saxon weaknesses meant they surrendered after the Battle of Hastings?

Although the Anglo-Saxons were in a strong position to fight on after the Battle of Hastings *(p.38)*, they were also weak in some important ways.

- William might have been able to cut London off from help from the north. He was also experienced in sieges.
- Edgar and the earls could not agree about the best course of action.
- The Battle of Hastings *(p.38)* had been a crushing defeat, in which many of England's best warriors were killed.
- Some earls saw William's victory as God's will, and therefore to be accepted rather than challenged.

How did the strengths of the Normans lead to English surrender after the Battle of Hastings?

William and the Normans had some advantages after their victory at Hastings.

- William seized the treasury of England, which meant he had the means to reward his followers while Edgar did not.
- William's effective leadership kept his troops going, despite their illness and battle-weariness.
- His methods of intimidating the Anglo-Saxons were effective. All the towns and villages the Normans destroyed were quick to surrender.

What Norman weaknesses might have meant the English didn't have to surrender after the Battle of Hastings.

After the Battle of Hastings *(p.38)*, the Normans had some problems to contend with.

- They were deep in enemy territory, with no secure defences or base.
- The Witan and the leaders of the Church had chosen their new king, which made William's claim obsolete.
- He had fewer soldiers than the potential numbers of the fyrd.
- Sickness had hit the Norman troops at Dover.

WILLIAM'S REWARDS TO HIS FOLLOWERS

William had persuaded his followers to fight for him. Now he was in control of England, he had to reward them.

Did William I reward his followers?

William I rewarded his supporters generously.

Why did William reward his followers?

William needed to reward his army, as they had travelled to England to fight for him, and had won him a great victory. He also needed their continued support to prevent trouble from the Anglo-Saxons.

How did William gain the land and money for rewards after 1066?

William gained the land and money to reward his supporters in various ways.

- He confiscated the royal treasury at Winchester.
- He set a heavy tax to raise funds from the Anglo-Saxons.

- ✅ He declared that all of the land in England belonged to him. He also took land off anyone who had fought against him at Hastings.

How did William I reward his Norman supporters?

William had persuaded Normans and mercenaries to join his army with the promise of wealth if they won.

- ✅ He kept about a fifth of the Godwinsons' and Edward's lands for himself, but granted the rest of it to his followers.
- ✅ His half-brother Odo, Bishop of Bayeux, received all of Kent.
- ✅ William FitzOsbern, William's relative and advisor, was granted large areas of Hampshire and the west, along with the Isle of Wight.
- ✅ Roger de Montgomery, who ruled Normandy while William was away, was made Earl of Shrewsbury. He also received land in Essex and Sussex.

How did William reward his Anglo-Saxon supporters?

The Anglo-Saxons who swore loyalty to William hoped for a share in the Godwin family's lands, but that went to William's supporters.

- ✅ Earls such as Edwin and Morcar were allowed to keep their earldoms.
- ✅ Bishops such as Ealdred kept their positions.
- ✅ The Northumbrian Gospatric was made earl of northern Northumbria after paying a heavy tax to William.
- ✅ William also gained support by promising marriage alliances. For example, he promised that Edwin could marry his daughter.

THE MARCHER EARLDOMS

The Marcher earldoms were created to help protect Norman England from attacks by the Welsh and the Scots.

What were the Marcher earldoms?

The Marcher earldoms were new earldoms created by William along the border of Wales, to prevent the threat of Welsh attacks that Edward the Confessor had suffered.

Where were the Marcher earldoms?

The Marcher earldoms were created on the Welsh frontier.

- ✅ The earldom of Chester was created next to north Wales.
- ✅ The earldom of Shrewsbury was situated alongside the Welsh midlands.
- ✅ The earldom of Hereford was adjacent to south Wales.

Who were the Marcher earldoms awarded to?

William awarded the Marcher earldoms to some of his closest supporters and advisers.

- ✅ Hugh d'Avranches, whose father had contributed 60 ships to William's fleet, was made Earl of Chester.
- ✅ Roger de Montgomery, who ruled Normandy while William was away, was made Earl of Shrewsbury.
- ✅ William's right-hand man, William FitzOsbern, was made Earl of Hereford.

What was significant about the size of the Marcher earldoms?

The Marcher earldoms were smaller than Anglo-Saxon earldoms, which made them easier to control, but also meant that the Marcher earls were not as powerful and important as the king.

What rights did the Marcher earldoms have?
The Marcher earls could establish Norman churches instead of Anglo-Saxon ones, and create towns (boroughs) and markets. These were powers normally reserved only for the king. They encouraged Normans to move into the areas.

What laws could the Marcher earldoms make?
The sheriffs in the Marcher earldoms were answerable to the earl, rather than directly to the king. This gave the Marcher earls almost complete control over the courts and law and order in their regions.

What taxes did they pay in the Marcher earldoms?
Unlike other English earls, Marcher earls did not have to pay tax to the king on their land. This was a reward for loyalty, but also to encourage development of towns and defences.

What happened with castles in the Marcher earldoms?
Unlike the rest of England, the Marcher earls could build *(p.75)* castles wherever they were needed, without asking permission from the king. This meant that they could control the area and attack the Welsh if necessary.

How powerful were the Marcher earldoms?
The Marcher earls controlled the frontier and had the autonomy to deal with trouble quickly and decisively. However, they still owed allegiance to the king, had to provide military service for him, and could not try people for high treason.

MOTTE AND BAILEY CASTLES
The Norman use of castles was an important factor in the way they demonstrated their power and control over England.

What were castles like in Norman times?
It is estimated that William built as many as 1,000 castles as a way of keeping control in England.

What were motte and bailey castles like?
The earliest Norman castles were known as motte and bailey castles. The motte was a large mound of earth that was topped with a keep, a wooden tower. The motte was surrounded by a bailey that contained the stables, barracks and kitchens.

What type of castles did the Normans build?
The Normans initially built motte and bailey castles. As time went on these were gradually rebuilt in stone.

Where were Norman castles built?
Castles were built in strategic locations such as key transport routes. They were also located where there was more likely to be unrest, so there were many castles on the Welsh frontier, as well as in Exeter, York and Nottingham.

What were the features of a motte and bailey castle?
Norman castles were known as motte and bailey castles, after their two key features - the motte and the bailey.
- ✓ The motte was a large mound of earth, about five to seven metres high.

- The keep was a strong wooden tower on top of the motte, that served as a lookout, an archers' stronghold, and the most secure defensive position in the castle.
- The keep was accessed by steps cut into the motte, or a bridge.
- The bailey surrounded the motte and contained the stables, barracks and kitchens.
- The bailey was protected by a strong wooden fence called a palisade.
- A deep ditch surrounded the bailey and the motte. Sometimes this was filled with water.
- Entry to the castle was controlled by a gatehouse.
- Sometimes a drawbridge was built over the ditch, which could be drawn up in case of an attack.

What were the advantages of Norman castles?

Motte and bailey castles had several advantages for the Normans.
- They were relatively quick and easy to build *(p.75)*. With peasant labour, they could be constructed within weeks. Basic fortifications could even be completed within days, if necessary.
- They were new in England (although common in Normandy and other parts of Europe), which made them unfamiliar and intimidating to the Anglo-Saxons.
- They served as a symbol of Norman power.
- They provided a secure base for the lord and his soldiers.

What were the effects of Norman castles?

Castles had a huge effect on the surrounding areas.
- They dominated the skyline and intimidated the Anglo-Saxons living nearby.
- In troublesome areas, they were spaced 20 miles apart. Norman soldiers could march 20 miles in a day, so this allowed them to deal with unrest quickly.
- Tens or hundreds of Anglo-Saxon homes might be destroyed to build *(p.75)* them - especially in towns - and local labour was used to build them.

How were Norman castles different to burhs?

Like the Anglo-Saxon burhs, castles were fortified against attack. However, there were some key differences between them.
- Burhs enclosed a whole town, but castles were smaller and therefore easier to defend.
- Burhs were public, and protected everyone in the area. Castles were private and only for the lord, his servants and soldiers.
- It was easier to set burhs on fire, as the houses had thatched roofs which burnt easily. Although castles were made of wood, they had earth fortifications and the additional height of the motte to protect them from fire.
- Burhs were for the protection of Anglo-Saxons, while castles were built to control them.

DID YOU KNOW?

Windsor Castle in Berkshire was originally built around 1070. It is the longest continuously occupied palace in Europe.

REBELLIONS AGAINST WILLIAM

Despite his victory at Hastings, it took William some years to fully pacify his new kingdom. He had to face a number of rebellions by his Saxon subjects.

What were the Anglo-Saxons rebellions against the Normans?
As William attempted to establish control over England, many Anglo-Saxons weren't prepared to accept Norman rule. In several places, this discontent turned into rebellion, where the people rose up and fought against the Normans.

When were the main Anglo-Saxon rebellions against the Normans?
There were a number of Anglo-Saxon rebellions against William while he was establishing control over England in the years 1066-1071.
- Rebellions in Kent, Northumbria, and on the Welsh border, in 1067.
- A rebellion in Exeter in 1068. William besieged Exeter, and prevented a further outbreak by granting the rebels concessions.
- A major rebellion in the north, led by Edwin and Morcar, in 1068.
- A major rebellion in the north, led by Edgar Aetheling, in 1069.
- A major rebellion in East Anglia, led by Hereward the Wake, in 1070-71.

EDWIN AND MORCAR'S REBELLION, 1068

Even though he allowed the Saxon earls, Edwin and Morcar, to keep their land and titles, William had to deal with their rebellion.

What was Edwin and Morcar's rebellion?
In 1067, William returned to Normandy, taking with him Edwin, Morcar, Edgar Aetheling and other Anglo-Saxon lords, as well as English treasure. On their return in 1068, Edwin and Morcar fled north and led a rebellion *(p.47)* against William.

When was the rebellion of Edwin and Morcar?
Edwin and Morcar rebelled in the year 1068.

What was the importance of Edwin and Morcar's rebellion?
This was the first major rebellion *(p.47)* against William. It encouraged the next phase of rebellions, which led to William using more brutal methods to crush subsequent revolts.

What were the causes of Edwin and Morcar's rebellion?
There were five main reasons why the lords rebelled.
- Edwin and Morcar were unhappy about the land that they had lost under William.
- The English lords who went with William to Normandy were resentful when they returned - perhaps because they realised that English wealth would be used to benefit Normandy.
- They resented William's heavy geld tax.
- They resented the castles that the Normans had built across England.
- They were alarmed by the brutality of Norman rule.

Why did Edwin lead the rebellion against the Normans with Morcar?
Edwin, Earl of Mercia, had 2 main complaints against William.
- ✅ His earldom in Mercia had been made smaller and less important than it previously had been.
- ✅ William had gone back on his promise that Edwin could marry his daughter.

Why did Morcar lead a rebellion against William I with Edwin?
Morcar had three main reasons for rebelling:
- ✅ Morcar resented the reduction of his landholding in Northumbria, and with it, his money and power.
- ✅ Parts of Northumbria had been given to one of Tostig's thegns, Copsig, who had submitted to William's rule.
- ✅ Control over parts of Yorkshire had been granted to Maerleswein.

How did land loss cause Edwin and Morcar's rebellion?
The Normans who had come to England with William took land from the Anglo-Saxons, which William allowed.

How did Norman brutality cause Edwin and Morcar's rebellion?
Odo and William FitzOsbern had unlawfully seized lands, and their soldiers had been allowed to behave brutally, even raping Anglo-Saxon women.

Why did resentment over castles lead to Edwin and Morcar's rebellion in 1069?
Norman castles were resented for several reasons:
- ✅ They represented Norman power and control.
- ✅ They often involved the destruction of Anglo-Saxon homes.
- ✅ The Normans commandeered resources from the surrounding areas to build *(p.75)* the castles.

Why did Norman taxes lead to Edwin and Morcar's rebellion in 1069?
The heavy geld tax that William introduced in late 1066 was resented.

Who was involved in Edwin and Morcar's rebellion?
The 1068 rebellion *(p.47)* in the north involved a number of Anglo-Saxon lords.
- ✅ Brothers Edwin, Earl of Mercia, and Morcar, Earl of Northumbria, were its leaders.
- ✅ Bleddyn, Lord of Powys in Wales.
- ✅ Maerleswein, Sheriff of Yorkshire.
- ✅ Earl Waltheof and Earl Gospatric of Northumbria.
- ✅ Edgar Aetheling, great-nephew of Edward the Confessor.

How did William respond to Edwin and Morcar's rebellion in 1068 - 1069?
William responded to the rebellion *(p.47)* swiftly, with a show of great force.
- ✅ He went north with his army, building *(p.75)* castles as they marched.
- ✅ They went to Warwick, a key town in Mercia, and built a castle there.
- ✅ They also built a castle in Nottingham.

How did the rebels react after Edwin and Morcar's rebellion?
The rebellion *(p.47)* disintegrated quickly when William took action.

- Edwin and Morcar surrendered after William took control of Warwick. William pardoned them, but kept them at his court where he could keep an eye on them. They escaped again in 1071.
- York sent hostages to William after he took Nottingham, as did the Northumbrian rebels.
- Edgar and other rebel leaders fled to Malcolm III in Scotland.

Why did Edwin and Morcar's rebellion fail?

There are a number of possible reasons why Edwin and Morcar's rebellion (p.47) failed.

- It may have been a test to see how William responded. The rebels could have been waiting for a better opportunity.
- It is possible that the rebels were not clear or united about what they wanted. Edwin and Morcar may have just wanted their land back.
- The escape of rebel leaders, including Edgar Aetheling, to Scotland, created a new rebel base which was important in 1069.
- Ultimately, William's show of force and efficient castle-building was an effective way of regaining control.

EDGAR AETHELING'S REBELLION, 1069

Edgar Aetheling continued to challenge William and led a rebellion against Norman rule in 1069.

What was Edgar Aetheling's rebellion in 1069?

In 1069 there was another rebellion (p.47) against William, led by Edgar Aetheling, which started with the murder of Robert Cumin, one of William's supporters.

Who led the Edgar Aetheling rebellion in 1069?

Edgar Aetheling, great-nephew of Edward the Confessor, led the rebellion (p.47), but he was joined by others.

- Malcolm III of Scotland, who was married to Edgar's sister, supported him.
- King Sweyn of Denmark sent a fleet and army, led by his brother Asbjorn, which joined Edgar.

What was important about Edgar Aetheling's rebellion of 1069?

Edgar's rebellion (p.47) was important because it led to the Harrying of the North and marked a change in William's strategy in dealing with rebellions.

Why was Robert Cumin killed in Edgar Aetheling's rebellion of 1069?

One of the rebels' targets was Robert Cumin, a supporter of William.

- William chose Cumin to replace Gospatric as earl of northern Northumbria, after Gospatric's betrayal in 1068.
- Cumin and a large force of his men attacked and looted towns in northern Northumbria in January 1069.
- The Bishop of Durham warned Cumin that this would cause resentment, but Cumin ignored him.
- A group of Northumbrians surprised Cumin's men, and killed them in the streets of Durham.
- Cumin hid in the bishop's house, but the rebels set fire to it, and killed him when he ran out.

What happened in York during Edgar Aetheling's rebellion of 1068 - 1069?

Shortly after the murder of Robert Cumin, there was a similar revolt (p.47) in York.

- The uprising (p.47) began when rebels killed the Norman governor of York and many Norman soldiers.
- They were joined by Edgar Aetheling and his rebels from Scotland.

How did William react to the uprising in York in Edgar Aetheling's rebellion of 1068 - 1069?
William took a large army to York very quickly in February, and dealt with the rebellion *(p.47)* there.
- ☑ His troops devastated York as they hunted for the rebels.
- ☑ Edgar Aetheling escaped back to Scotland.
- ☑ William built a new castle, and put William FitzOsbern in charge of it.
- ☑ He then returned to Winchester for Easter celebrations.

How did the Vikings get involved in Edgar Aetheling's rebellion of 1068 - 1069?
In September 1069, William's troubles worsened when a Danish force joined Edgar's Anglo-Saxon rebels and looted York.
- ☑ The Viking forces that joined Edgar's rebellion *(p.47)* in 1069 increased the pressure on William's rule.
- ☑ King Sweyn of Denmark assembled a large fleet..
- ☑ The Danes raided the east coast, meeting up with Edgar's troops and co-ordinating their attacks.
- ☑ The combined army marched on York.
- ☑ The Norman army accidentally set the city on fire in their attempts to defend it.
- ☑ They then went out to meet the Anglo-Danish rebels, and were slaughtered.
- ☑ Both castles in York were destroyed and the Danish ships sailed home full of English riches.
- ☑ As William travelled the north hunting down the rebels, news of other rebellions came from Shrewsbury and Chester.

Why did Edgar Aetheling's rebellion of 1069 fail?
Although William's rule was under pressure, the Normans managed to maintain power, for a number of reasons.
- ☑ The rebels retreated when William led troops into an area.
- ☑ The Anglo-Danish army split up after reaching York, instead of marching south.
- ☑ William was able to stop the Viking attacks by paying off the Danes.

Was William worried by the Danes during Edgar Aetheling's rebellion of 1068 -1069?
The Danes were a worry for William, for a variety of reasons.
- ☑ They were far more experienced sailors than the Normans.
- ☑ There was a possibility that they would be more welcome in the Danelaw *(p.16)* than the Normans were.
- ☑ William believed that they would keep raiding and then retreating until the Norman troops were exhausted.

How did William react to the Viking rebels during Edgar Aetheling's rebellion of 1069?
William marched his troops up north to put down the Anglo-Danish rebellion *(p.47)*, but the rebels fled. He therefore changed his tactics.
- ☑ He paid the Danes a large sum of money to leave.
- ☑ He began a campaign of total destruction in the north of England - the 'Harrying of the North'.

THE HARRYING OF THE NORTH, 1069-1070

Three years after Hastings, William had lost patience with rebellious Saxons. In the winter of 1069-70 he decided to show them exactly what the price of rebellion was.

What was the Harrying of the North?
'Harrying' means to devastate a place. In 1069, William decided to deal with uprisings in the north with an event that became known as 'The Harrying of the North'. Norman soldiers stormed villages, killing many people, burning fields, and destroying livestock and food stores.

When was the Harrying of the North?
The Harrying of the North began in the winter of 1069 and continued into 1070.

What was the importance of the Harrying of the North?
The Harrying of the North was important because it marked a turning point in William's strategy for dealing with rebellions. The consequences made it difficult to continue resistance against William.

Why did the Normans harry the north?
It is possible that William ordered the Harrying of the North in a fit of rage - there is evidence that he regretted it afterwards. However, at the time there were several other reasons for his decision.
- Many Normans, including the Norman earl Robert Cumin, had been killed by rebels.
- The guerrilla tactics of the rebels meant that William was unable to meet them in open battle. Instead, they took refuge in nearby villages. The Harrying of the North made this impossible.
- The Danish heritage of Anglo-Saxons in the north meant that their loyalty might be swayed by Danish invaders.
- The rebellions in the north triggered other rebellions across England.

What were the short-term effects of the Harrying of the North?
The effects of the Harrying of the North in the short-term were horrific. An estimated 100,000 to 150,000 people were either killed, died of starvation in the resulting famine, or were displaced as refugees to other parts of the kingdom.

What were the long-term effects of the Harrying of the North?
The effects of the Harrying of the North lasted for many years.
- There were no further uprisings in Northumbria.
- 16 years later, the Domesday Book *(p.73)* showed that one third of Yorkshire remained wasteland, and that there were as many as 150,000 fewer people in the area.
- The Danes no longer used the Danelaw *(p.16)* as a beachhead for their invasions, and instead attacked in East Anglia.
- William decided to replace the remaining Anglo-Saxon nobility, rather than trying to work with them any more.
- The Harrying was widely criticised, including by the pope. William gave a lot of time and money to the Church as penance (to make amends) for his actions.

How many people were killed in the Harrying of the North?
It is unsure how many people were killed or died of starvation as a result of the Harrying of the North, but estimates range between 80,000 and 100,000 people.

> **DID YOU KNOW?**
>
> **Two facts about the Harrying of the North:**
> - ✓ The Anglo-Norman writer, Orderic Vitalis, said that 100,000 people were killed or starved to death in the Harrying of the North. This was as much as 5% of the population.
> - ✓ Fifteen years later, one third of Yorkshire was still described as 'waste'.

HEREWARD THE WAKE AND REBELLION, 1070-1071

Despite the destruction of the Harrying of the North, William faced a new rebellion in 1070-71, this time in East Anglia.

What was the rebellion of Hereward the Wake?
After the Harrying of the North, Hereward the Wake began a rebellion *(p.47)* in the Fens of East Anglia, supported by the Danes who had returned to England.

When was the rebellion of Hereward the Wake?
Hereward the Wake was active against the Normans in 1070, which is when the uprising *(p.47)* at Ely occurred.

Who was involved in the 1070 uprising?
The 1070 uprising in Ely was another Anglo-Viking uprising *(p.47)*.
- ✓ King Sweyn led his Danish fleet back to England.
- ✓ He made an alliance with a local rebel leader called Hereward the Wake.

Why did Hereward the Wake rebel?
Hereward had been a local thegn who fought abroad, before coming home to find that his land had been given to a Norman lord.
- ✓ The Bishop of Peterborough had been replaced by a Norman called Turold.
- ✓ Hereward and the other East Anglian rebels fought a guerrilla war against the Normans.

Where was the 1070 rebellion?
The rising in 1070-1071 was centred in Ely, in the Fens of East Anglia.

How did William deal with guerrilla warfare during the rebellion of Hereward the Wake?
William had a number of methods for dealing with the guerrilla tactics of the rebels.
- ✓ He responded rapidly with a large force to stamp out resistance.
- ✓ He put trusted supporters in place to keep control of areas, once rebellions had been stamped out.
- ✓ He established castles in troubled areas.
- ✓ Ultimately, he decided that the remaining Anglo-Saxon lords needed to be removed from power.
- ✓ As a sign of desperation, however, William was said to have employed a witch to curse Hereward.
- ✓ As he had in 1069, William paid large sums of money to the Danish invaders to go away.

How did William deal with discontent during the rebellion of 1070?
William dealt with unhappy troops by offering them more rewards for their service. He raised the money and land for this by further taxation and land confiscation.

How did William deal with Edgar Aetheling after the rebellion of 1070?
Edgar Aetheling had a better claim to the throne than William. William countered this by paying special attention to royal ceremonies and celebrations. He made sure that he was seen in public as the king.

What happened in Ely during the rebellion of 1070?
From 1070-1071, William had to deal with the combined force of the Danes, Hereward the Wake and Earl Morcar.
- In 1070 and 1071, the Danes and Anglo-Saxon rebels raided Peterborough Abbey, and the Danes sailed away with its wealth.
- Hereward was joined by Earl Morcar, and they prepared to defend Ely.
- The Normans managed to retake Ely, possibly by bribing monks to show them the way through the marshes.
- Morcar was captured and imprisoned for life. Hereward escaped and was never heard of again.

THE EARLS' REVOLT
In 1075, William faced a different kind of rebellion. This time it was his Norman lords who rebelled.

What was the Earls' Revolt?
In 1075, William faced another rebellion (p.47). This time, however, the rebels were his own men - the Normans.

When was the Earls' Revolt?
The Earls' Revolt (p.47) occurred in 1075.

What were the aims of the Earls' Revolt?
The leaders of the Earls' Revolt (p.47) planned to overthrow William and divide England into three parts, shared between them.

Who was involved in the Earls' Revolt?
There were three main figures in the Earls' Revolt (p.47), along with other supporters.
- Ralph de Gael, Earl of East Anglia - a Norman.
- Roger de Breteuil, Earl of Hereford - a Norman.
- Waltheof, Earl of Northumbria - an Anglo-Saxon.
- A fleet of Danish invaders, led by Sweyn's son Cnut, was assembled to help the rebels.
- Brittany and France, rivals of Normandy, were both prepared to help the earls in the revolt (p.47).

What were the causes of the Earls' Revolt?
The earls are believed to have had a number of reasons for rebelling.
- They resented the loss of their lands, privileges and power.
- William was away in Normandy at the time, leaving Archbishop Lanfranc in charge.
- They had powerful allies in the form of the Danes, the French and the Bretons.

- ✅ They believed that the Anglo-Saxons were prepared to rebel.

Why did Ralph de Gael lead the Earls' Revolt?
Not much is known about Ralph de Gael's motives in rebelling against William, but it is likely that he resented having less wealth and power than his father had possessed. He also had strong links to Brittany.

Why did Roger de Breteuil lead the Earls' Revolt?
Roger de Breteuil was the son of William's most trusted advisor, but he was angry when William reduced his land in the Marcher earldom *(p.44)* and introduced his own sheriffs to the area.

Why did Earl Waltheof lead the Earls' Revolt?
Waltheof was invited to join the rebellion *(p.47)* at the wedding of de Gael to de Breteuil's sister, Emma. He was a former rebel with links to Denmark. However, he may have been a double agent in the revolt.

How did the Earls' Revolt begin?
The revolt *(p.47)* began when the rebels began to strengthen the defences of the castles in Hereford and East Anglia, and built up their troops ready to march.

Why was the wedding important in Earls' Revolt?
The wedding symbolised unity between de Gael and de Breteuil's families. It was attended by many important members of the aristocracy, and was where Waltheof was invited to join the plot.

What problems did the leaders face in the Earls' Revolt?
The leaders of the Earls' Revolt *(p.47)* faced a number of problems.
- ✅ The Anglo-Saxons did not support them.
- ✅ Waltheof changed his mind and informed Archbishop Lanfranc, who sent men to East Anglia and Hereford to find out what was going on.
- ✅ Bishop Wulfstan of Worcester and the abbot of Evesham used their troops to prevent de Breteuil from leaving Herefordshire, while de Gael was blocked in East Anglia.
- ✅ William returned to England.
- ✅ The Danish fleet of 200 ships arrived too late to help the rebels. Instead of facing William in battle, Cnut raided the east coast and then returned home.

What did Lanfranc do in the Earls' Revolt?
Archbishop Lanfranc, who had been left in charge of England while William was away, took several actions during the Earl's Revolt *(p.47)*.
- ✅ He sent men to East Anglia and Hereford to report on the rebels' actions.
- ✅ He wrote to Roger de Breteuil to remind him of his loyalty to William.
- ✅ He excommunicated de Breteuil when he didn't stop the revolt *(p.47)*.
- ✅ He made preparations to prevent the revolt *(p.47)*.

How did William react to the Earls' Revolt?
William responded severely to the Earl's revolt *(p.47)*.
- ✅ He tricked Waltheof into returning to England after he fled abroad, then imprisoned and executed him, despite his role in informing on the rebels.
- ✅ He had de Gael's Breton supporters blinded or banished, but allowed Emma safe passage to Brittany after she took refuge in Norwich castle.

- ☑ He imprisoned Roger de Breteuil for life.
- ☑ He attacked de Gael's castle in Brittany, but was forced to retreat after France sent troops to help Ralph.

 What was the importance of the Earls' Revolt?

The Earls' Revolt (p.47) was significant for William and England in a number of ways:

- ☑ It showed that, having conquered England, William now had to watch his own supporters for treachery.
- ☑ Anglo-Saxons, such as Bishop Wulfstan, supported William rather than the rebels.
- ☑ William had Waltheof executed after the rebellion (p.47), which showed that he was still ruthless about Anglo-Saxon rebellion.
- ☑ The failure of Cnut's Danish invasion marked the end of the Danish attacks on England. At the time, however, William saw it as a serious threat.

WILLIAM I

William, Duke of Normandy became King William I of England. He was also known as William the Conqueror.

 Who was William the Conqueror?

William was the Duke of Normandy, and became King of England after the Battle of Hastings (p 38) in 1066. By the time William conquered England, he had survived numerous assassination attempts as a boy and had years of military experience.

 Why did William I think he should be king?

There were a number of reasons why William felt he had a strong claim to the throne.

- ☑ He was related to Edward the Confessor through his great-aunt, Emma of Normandy, who was Edward's mother.
- ☑ Before becoming king, Edward had spent over twenty years in exile in Normandy. So there was an established relationship between them.
- ☑ William had helped Edward in 1051, when Earl Godwin rebelled. William claimed that, in return, Edward had promised him the throne.
- ☑ William was an experienced ruler, and an experienced and successful warrior.
- ☑ William claimed that Harold Godwinson had sworn an oath to support his claim, in 1064.

 What were the weaknesses of William I's claim to the throne?

Although William felt he had a strong claim to the throne, there were arguments against it.

- ☑ William's blood relationship to Edward was not strong.
- ☑ Many of the Saxons disliked the idea of a foreign king. They had objected to the number of Normans that Edward had invited to England in the 1050s.
- ☑ Edward had nominated Harold Godwinson on his deathbed, and the Saxons believed that deathbed promises held more weight than earlier promises.
- ☑ Although Harold Godwinson did not deny swearing an oath to William in 1064, he denied that he had sworn the oath to support William's claim.

 How effective was William I's leadership in the Battle of Hastings?

Although the outcome of the Battle of Hastings (p.38) was partly determined by luck, William's leadership made the Norman chances of victory stronger. His strengths included discipline, timing, preparation, brutality, and intelligence.

How did William I use discipline at the Battle of Hastings?
William demonstrated a good ability to discipline his troops before and during the Battle of Hastings *(p.38)*.
- ✅ William had to keep his army and fleet ready and waiting on the French coast for the entire summer.
- ✅ The Norman troops did not loot or steal food from the surrounding Norman countryside during the long summer.

 Did William I time his attack on England well?
William knew that eventually Harold Godwinson would have to disband the fyrd to gather the harvest. He prepared to sail as soon as he heard that this had happened, and caught Harold unawares.

 Was William I's attack on England in 1066 ambitious?
William's plans for the invasion of England were very ambitious and included the transport of hundreds of destriers by ship.

 How much preparation did William I make for the invasion of England?
William demonstrated thorough preparation for the invasion of England in a number of ways.
- ✅ The Normans took pieces of a castle over the Channel with them, and used it to transform an old Iron Age fort in Hastings into a simple defence.
- ✅ William organised for the transport of the Norman destriers using flat-bottomed ships, as the Norman horses had been especially bred for battle.
- ✅ William had excellent information from his spies, who told him what Harold was doing in England, and allowed him to meet the Anglo-Saxons at Hastings.

 Were William I's troops brutal to the Anglo-Saxons in 1066?
Although the Norman troops had been well-disciplined in Normandy, William allowed them to loot and destroy English villages. This tactic enraged Harold and encouraged him to leave London.

 How did intelligence help William I's invasion?
William had good information from his spies (known as intelligence) about the actions of Harold and the Anglo-Saxon army *(p.19)*, and used it to make good leadership decisions.
- ✅ The Normans were not surprised by Harold's Anglo-Saxon troops, as he had hoped, and were instead able to sneak up on them early on the morning of the battle.
- ✅ William's knowledge of the Anglo-Saxons before the invasion allowed him to time the voyage after Harold had disbanded the fyrd.

 What were William I's tactics in the Battle of Hastings?
Because he had different types of soldiers, William was able to employ a variety of tactics in the Battle of Hastings *(p.38)*.
- ✅ Feigning retreat.
- ✅ Using a combination of infantry, archers and cavalry.

 Why did William I have an advantage at the Battle of Hastings?
Although Harold held the top of the hill, with his shield wall in a strong defensive position, William was able to make use of some tactical advantages. These included:
- ✅ Soldiers with a variety of fighting styles.
- ✅ His cavalry.
- ✅ Archers.
- ✅ Well-disciplined troops.

When was William I crowned king of England?
William was crowned in Westminster Abbey by Archbishop Ealdred of York, on Christmas Day 1066.

What powers did William I have?
As the first Norman king of England, William had economic, legal, military, social and religious powers.
- He controlled coins and the currency.
- He made all the laws.
- He could raise taxes - this was called 'levying the geld'.
- He owned all the land, and could grant it and take it away.
- He had military power, made up of knights provided by the tenants-in-chief.
- He could appoint important churchmen.
- He would call a meeting of the Witan to advise him.
- He issued laws and instructions by using royal writs.
- He held oath-taking ceremonies to gain the loyalty of his landholders.
- He wore the crown to show his power and position to the people.

How did William I's military power help him?
William was a strong, skilful and ruthless military leader, and this helped him to claim the crown in England.
- He was able to win the Battle of Hastings *(p.38)* and crush rebellions.
- It won the respect of the Anglo-Saxons, who admired great warriors. Many joined his side against the rebels.
- People at the time believed that his victories were a sign that he was favoured by God.

How did William I prove his legitimacy as king?
It was important to William that the Anglo-Saxons saw him as the rightful - or legitimate - king.
- He stressed that he was the rightful heir to Edward the Confessor's throne because Edward had promised it to him, because he was related to Edward, and because Harold had broken his oath.
- At his coronation he promised to uphold Edward's laws, and protect the Church.
- He made sure that he was seen wearing the crown in public at least three times a year. These included at religious festivals and in important places.
- He was crowned by Ealdred, the Archbishop of York. Normally the Archbishop of Canterbury crowned the king, but Archbishop Stigand was corrupt, and therefore was not considered appropriate.
- He made sure that images of his portrait were put onto coins so that everyone could see he was the king.

How did William I use ceremonies to show his power?
William made sure that he appeared as the true and rightful king, wearing his crown at important times and places.
- At important religious festivals, such as Christmas and Easter.
- At important places in England, such as Westminster and Gloucester.
- He also wore his crown after putting down Edgar Aetheling's rebellion *(p.47)* in 1069, in the ruins of York.

How did William I control money?
William took control of the minting of coins, which had his portrait on them.

How did royal writs give William I power?
Royal writs were official documents and proclamations from the king, affixed with his seal. William used them to spread his commands across the country. To begin with he issued writs in English, to show continuity from Edward's reign.

How did William I travel to maintain his power?
William travelled England frequently with his court and met with officials and important families. It made him more familiar to the people and allowed him to see what was happening throughout his kingdom.

Why did the land make William I powerful?
Owning land directly made William more powerful, as it meant that everyone ultimately relied on loyalty to him to keep their land. The link between king and landholding was much stronger than in Anglo-Saxon times.

How did oath-taking increase William I's power?
Oath-taking was making a solemn promise, and was taken very seriously by the Anglo-Saxons. William held huge oath-taking ceremonies in which men would swear to serve him faithfully.

What sort of person was William I?
William's personality seems full of contradictions, but this may have been the effect of his reputation as the conqueror and ruler of England.
- ✅ He was clearly tough and determined.
- ✅ He was the illegitimate son of Robert, duke of Normandy, and survived many assassination attempts while a boy.
- ✅ He was warlike and ruthless, showing excellent leadership and strategy.
- ✅ He was very religious, and apparently repented on his deathbed the violence he had caused.
- ✅ He focused very strongly on being accepted as the legitimate heir of Edward the Confessor, rather than merely an invader in England.
- ✅ He loved his wife Matilda very much, and wept for days when she died in 1083.

How many children did William I have?
William and Matilda had at least nine children.

What was William I's relationship with his children?
William had a difficult relationship with his eldest son, Robert, partly because Robert wanted more power than William was prepared to give him.

When did William I die?
William died in 1087.
- ✅ In July 1087, William led a raid in France but was thrown from the saddle of his horse. By this time he was very fat, and it caused serious internal injuries.
- ✅ He died after several weeks of suffering.
- ✅ On his death, the nobility fled to secure their castles from attack while the servants stole everything they could.

What happened at William I's funeral?
At William's funeral his servants tried to squeeze his body into a stone tomb, but it burst and smelled so bad everyone had to leave the cathedral. This was seen as a bad omen, indicating God's anger against him.

Who succeeded William I?
Because William was on his death-bed for a while, he had time to decide who should take the throne after him.
- ☑ He decided that his eldest son, Robert, should inherit the dukedom of Normandy.
- ☑ He wanted his favourite son, William Rufus, to be king of England, but decided to leave it in the hands of God.
- ☑ William Rufus left for England before his father died, with a letter from William to Lanfranc. Lanfranc crowned him William II in September 1087.

ROBERT CURTHOSE
When William died, the title Duke of Normandy passed to his eldest son, Robert.

Who was Robert Curthose?
William's eldest son Robert was known as Robert Curthose, meaning 'short trousers'. This unflattering nickname was given to him in childhood, possibly by William. He had a number of disagreements with his father and tried to take the crown of England from his brother, William Rufus.

Why did Robert Curthose argue with William I?
Robert Curthose spent the years 1077 to 1080 effectively at war with his father. This was because he wanted more power than William was prepared to give him.
- ☑ In 1077, Robert and his army tried to take control of Rouen Castle after Robert's brothers played a prank on him and he felt William didn't punish them harshly enough.
- ☑ Robert fled to Flanders and was given a castle on Normandy's borders by the King of France. Robert launched raids against his father's land.
- ☑ William raised an army against him, but Matilda secretly sent him money, which caused a huge argument between them.
- ☑ They fought each other in battle in 1079. Robert knocked William off his horse, then gave him his own horse and ordered him to retreat. William was humiliated.
- ☑ Matilda organised a meeting between them in 1080. William made Robert the heir to Normandy again.

Why did Robert Curthose rebel against his brother?
Robert became Duke of Normandy when William the Conqueror died, but he wanted the throne of England which had gone to his brother, William Rufus.
- ☑ Norman custom generally stated that the eldest son inherited all his father's estates.
- ☑ Many Norman lords owned land in England and Normandy, and would have preferred a single ruler over both.
- ☑ His uncle, Bishop Odo, stirred up rebellion *(p.47)* on behalf of his claim, but Robert did not come to help him when he was besieged in Rochester Castle.

> **DID YOU KNOW?**
>
> **Three facts about Robert of Normandy:**
> - ✓ Robert took part in the First Crusade in the 1090s, although he left before the Crusaders reached Jerusalem in 1099.
> - ✓ Robert was imprisoned for 27 years. He was 83 years old when he died in 1134.
> - ✓ Robert's son, William Clito, argued until his death that he had a claim to the throne. He was just 25 years old when he died, in 1128.

WILLIAM RUFUS

William had named his second son, also called William, as his successor in the event of his own death. William II is usually known as William Rufus.

Who was William Rufus?

William II was known as William Rufus, possibly because of either his rosy cheeks or red hair. He faced serious challenges when he became king. William Rufus was the second of William the Conqueror's sons, and became King William II on his father's death.

What happened after William Rufus took power?

After his coronation, William Rufus faced uprisings by those who supported his brother, Robert Curthose. These included his uncle, Bishop Odo.

Why was William Rufus challenged as king?

There were a number of reasons William Rufus's reign was challenged:
- ✓ William's decision before his death seemed unclear and was open to interpretation.
- ✓ Robert Curthose was made Duke of Normandy. Lords with land in both England and Normandy didn't want to answer to two different rulers.
- ✓ Robert Curthose believed he should rule England, as he was William's eldest son.

How did Robert react to William Rufus' coronation?

William Rufus' brother, Robert Curthose, Duke of Normandy, also wanted to rule England and supported those who rebelled against Rufus.

What other revolts did William Rufus face?

As well as those by Odo and Robert, William Rufus had to deal with smaller rebellions.
- ✓ Raids in Somerset and Wiltshire by Robert de Mowbray.
- ✓ A revolt *(p.47)* led by Roger Bigod in Norwich and the sheriff of Leicester.
- ✓ Raids in Gloucester by William of Eu.
- ✓ Rebellions in the west led by the Marcher earls Robert de Montgomery and Roger de Lacy.

How did William Rufus win?

William Rufus used a number of effective tactics to overcome the rebellions.

- ✅ He raised an army, but took the money their lords had given the knights to live on and sent the soldiers home.
- ✅ He then used the money to bribe barons in eastern Normandy, forcing Robert to agree to rule it alongside him.
- ✅ He promised to lower taxes, to end the forest laws, and to return to Edward the Confessor's laws. This removed the complaints behind the rebellions. However, Rufus did not deliver any of these promises.

Who succeeded William Rufus?
When William Rufus was killed in 1100 his youngest brother, Henry, became king.

BISHOP ODO
Bishop Odo of Bayeux was William's half-brother and played an important role in events of the time.

Who was Bishop Odo?
Bishop Odo was William's half-brother, and was awarded the earldom of Kent in England, as well as a number of other large estates.

What was Odo's relationship with William like?
Odo and William had the same mother, and probably grew up together. He lent 100 ships to William's invasion fleet and fought at the Battle of Hastings *(p.38)*.

How did Odo behave in England?
With William FitzOsbern, Odo was William's regent when he returned to Normandy in 1067. He was very powerful, unpopular with the Anglo-Saxons, and seems to have settled land disputes by himself. He was accused of making land-grabs.

Why did Odo get into trouble?
From 1076, it seems that William was less tolerant of Odo's behaviour.
- ✅ Archbishop Lanfranc took the Church's complaints against Odo to William, and in 1076 Odo was forced to hand back the land he had taken.
- ✅ In 1079, William sent Odo to Northumbria after attacks by the Scottish. Odo reportedly devastated Durham and ransacked the cathedral. He also robbed and extorted people.

Why was Odo sent to prison?
In 1082, Odo was imprisoned by William due to his greed and was not released until the king was on his deathbed.

How did Bishop Odo react to William Rufus?
Bishop Odo, freed from prison in 1087, joined the rebellion *(p.47)* to support Robert's claim as king. This may have been because he thought that Robert would be easier to control.
- ✅ Odo's brother, Robert of Mortain, also joined the rebellion. *(p.47)*
- ✅ Odo and his brother controlled large areas of the south of England.
- ✅ Odo and Robert of Mortain took refuge in Pevensey Castle, where William Rufus besieged them for six weeks.
- ✅ Both William Rufus' uncles were captured, but Odo managed to escape to Rochester Castle.
- ✅ He waited for help from his nephew, Robert, but it never came. Odo was eventually forced out of the castle by hunger and disease and was exiled.

> **DID YOU KNOW?**
>
> **Two facts about Odo of Bayeux:**
> - ✓ Even though he was a bishop, Odo fought at the Battle of Hastings.
> - ✓ Odo is thought to have commissioned the famous Bayeux Tapestry, which tells the story of the Battle of Hastings.

THE NORMANS AND LAND

After his victory at Hastings, William now 'owned' the whole of England. He set about transferring land from the remaining Saxon lords to his own Norman followers.

What happened to land under the Normans?

From 1066 until his death in 1087, William I oversaw the transfer of land from Anglo-Saxon to Norman ownership. This formed the basis of the feudal system *(p.65)*.

Why was land important for the Normans?

Land ownership provided food, money, followers and fighting men. It was therefore a source of power in England during William's reign.

What changed for the Normans about land-owning during William I's reign?

By the end of William's reign, much of the land in England had been redistributed to Normans, rather than Anglo-Saxons. Large portions were owned by the king and the Church, and estates were consolidated.

- ☑ The land had been redistributed to Normans, rather than Anglo-Saxons.
- ☑ Large portions were owned by the Church, which was controlled in England by the Normans.
- ☑ The king directly owned about one fifth of the land.
- ☑ Estates were consolidated, and a small number of lords held large amounts of land.

How much land did the Church own in Norman England?

A quarter of the land was owned by the Church, but the Normans held all the important Church positions.

Who had the most land in Norman England?

Although William was careful not to allow any individual more power than he had himself, he did consolidate land ownership among fewer people.

- ☑ By 1087, over half the land in England was held by around 190 tenants-in-chief. Of these, only two were Anglo-Saxons.
- ☑ Half the land held by the tenants-in-chief was held by 11 men. These included William's greatest supporters, such as Odo and William FitzOsbern.

How much land did the Anglo-Saxons get in Norman England?

By 1087, less than 5% of the land was held by Anglo-Saxons, and this was mostly in the form of smaller estates.

What happened to the thegns' land in Norman England?
There were about 4,000 thegns holding land in England when William took over in 1066. These were a potential threat to his rule.
- ✅ William took land from the thegns. By 1086 only four Anglo-Saxon thegns remained.
- ✅ Thegns were dependant on the Normans for the small amounts of land that they still held.
- ✅ The thegns' way of life was destroyed. Many went to Europe as mercenaries.

Why did William I change land-ownership in Norman England?
William had some good reasons for changing land-ownership in England after 1066.
- ✅ The rebellions of 1068-1071 showed that the Anglo-Saxons couldn't be trusted.
- ✅ He didn't want any one individual to have enough land to challenge his power.
- ✅ He had promised his followers land and riches if they fought for him at Hastings. He had to make good on that promise.

How was the land redistributed in Norman England?
The Normans used three main methods to transfer land-ownership from Anglo-Saxons to Normans.
- ✅ By forfeit. The king, who owned all land, could confiscate land taken from the disloyal and give it to new lords of his choice.
- ✅ New earldoms were made up of land that had belonged to other landholders, particularly to defend areas where there was unrest, such as the Welsh marches.
- ✅ Sometimes the Normans snatched land from Anglo-Saxons, through corrupt dealings or just by taking it. These land-grabs were illegal.

Which parts of English land did William I give to the Normans?
William was able to use his conquest and the rebellions to redistribute lands.
- ✅ After the Battle of Hastings *(p.38)*, William gave the Godwinson lands in the south and west of England to his followers.
- ✅ After the rebellions of 1068-1071, he redistributed the land in Mercia, Northumbria and East Anglia.

How did William I take control of the land in Norman England?
After 1071 William changed some of his lords' grants of land, so that they held more of it in the same place.
- ✅ Before 1071, forfeited Anglo-Saxon land *(p.18)* was passed to the Norman lords in bits and pieces, which meant they often held land in different regions.
- ✅ After 1071, William consolidated more blocks of land. This meant that there was a single authority in an area and was better for control.
- ✅ Before 1071, William had claimed that he was maintaining Anglo-Saxon traditions, but afterwards he took a more pragmatic approach to keep control.

CHANGES TO LANDHOLDING UNDER THE NORMANS

The main features of landholding in Norman England.

How did landholding change under the Normans?

The Normans introduced changes to landholding, including the way that land could be given out, the duties associated with holding it, and how secure and reliable it was.

How did landholding work under the Anglo-Saxons before the Normans changed them?

There were different types of tenure under the Anglo-Saxons.
- Bookland was when the lords granted the right to land to their followers, which was represented by a charter. This could be passed on to heirs or sold.
- Leases were when land was loaned to someone in return for money for a set amount of time.
- All landowners had to provide one fyrdman for every five hides, and pay geld tax.
- A tax was due to the lord when a new landholder inherited land from a dead one.

How did William I change landholding in Norman England?

There were some similarities, but some significant differences to landholding under the Normans.
- The king owned all the land, and this over-rode any previous agreements.
- Anglo-Saxons had to pay William money for the right to carry on using their land.
- Land granted by William to his followers did not need money to redeem. However, if they died without an heir then the land went back to the king. Any heirs had to pay a 'relief' (tax) to the king on inheriting their land.

Why did William change landholding in Norman England?

William had a number of reasons for changing methods of landholding in England.
- It gave him more control. Anyone who disobeyed him could be left without land.
- It earned him money, through the relief paid to redeem and inherit land.
- It made tenure less safe, which meant that tenants were more dependent on their lords and therefore less likely to rebel.

How much power did the tenants-in-chief have over landholding in Norman England?

The tenants-in-chief were extremely powerful in Norman England, and had firm control over land ownership in their areas.
- They became the lords of the thegns in the area.
- They could reallocate land if a thegn died.
- They could make their supporters 'heirs' to a thegn's land.
- They could take land away from anyone who acted against them.

How did landholding change things for the peasants in Norman England?

There were fewer ceorls (freemen) in Norman England, as the Norman lords increased rents which they could not afford. Many freemen therefore became un-free villeins.

THE FEUDAL SYSTEM

The social hierarchy of England was established through landholding in what has become known as the 'feudal system'.

What was the feudal system?
The feudal system is the name given to the way Norman society was structured.

What was the hierarchy of the feudal system?
The feudal system was a hierarchy of four main classes, or groups.
- ✅ The king was at the top of the system.
- ✅ Tenants-in-chief, important landholding lords, were less important than the king but more powerful than the under-tenants.
- ✅ Vassals, or under-tenants, who were often knights, were less important than the tenants-in-chief but more powerful than the peasants.
- ✅ Peasants were the lowest class in Norman society.

What did the king do in the feudal system?
The king had ultimate power in the feudal system. He owned all the land, and demanded loyalty from everyone who received it.

What did the tenants-in-chief do in the feudal system?
The tenants-in-chief received large areas of land from the king. In return, they promised to provide him with troops when they were needed. Land that was given under these circumstances was called a fief.

What did the vassals do in the feudal system?
The under-tenants, or vassals, received areas of land from the tenants-in-chief. In return, they gave military service to the tenants-in-chief.

What did the peasants do in the feudal system?
The peasants received small strips of land from their lords, which they farmed for themselves. In return, they had to do 'boon work' on the lord's land for some days of the week.

What about slaves in the feudal system in Norman England?
The Normans thought that slavery was wrong and gradually ended the practice in England.

What role did the Church have in the feudal system?
The Church played an important role in the feudal system.
- ✅ It was a major landholder and owned up to 25% of English land. Church tenants did boon work for the church, and the church collected the taxes for the king.
- ✅ Bishops owed the king military service, so the Church gave land to knights and made sure it could provide soldiers when needed.
- ✅ Bishops were the head of cathedrals and the area around them, known as the diocese. They helped to enforce the king's laws.
- ✅ Royal clerks were recruited from the Church to write legal documents, and important churchmen sometimes acted as judges.

> **DID YOU KNOW?**
>
> The Normans did not introduce the feudal system to England - it already existed in Saxon times - but adapted and developed it for their own purposes.

EXCHANGES IN THE FEUDAL SYSTEM

The feudal system worked on the basis of duties and obligations, by the king or lord as well as their tenants.

What was exchanged in the feudal system?

The feudal system *(p.65)* was a system of exchange of land, loyalty and labour.

How was land exchanged in the feudal system?

In the feudal system *(p.65)*, all of the land belonged to the king. This made his life simpler in a number of ways.
- Nobody could inherit land without making a relief payment to the king and swearing an oath of homage.
- The system of paying a relief encouraged loyalty to the king and also raised money for him.
- The king could reward favourites with low relief payments for their sons, and use high relief payments as a threat for rebellious ones.
- This system prevented any noble from gaining so much land that they could challenge the king.

How was homage exchanged in the feudal system?

The ceremony of homage was an important event in which the tenant-in-chief *(p.67)* knelt before the king and said 'I become your man'. He then swore on the Bible to remain loyal to the king for the rest of his life.

How was labour exchanged in the feudal system?

Peasants promised to work for their lord in return for enough land to support themselves.
- Sometimes this meant working on the lord's land to plough, sow and gather crops. This was known as 'boon work'.
- Sometimes this meant giving a set amount of their produce to the lord each year, as a form of tax.
- Peasants in towns had to do labour service for any land they farmed outside the town.

FORFEITURE

As well as gaining great benefit from the feudal system, the lords of England were kept in check by the threat of losing their land.

What was forfeiture?

If anyone failed to obey their lord, or did not provide the taxes or services they owed, they could be punished with the loss of their land. This was called forfeiture. For peasants it often meant that they became un-free villeins.

TENANTS-IN-CHIEF
William's rule in England was supported by his tenants-in-chief, the great lords of the kingdom

What were tenants in chief?
The tenants-in-chief were directly answerable to the king, and played an important role in Norman society. They were large landholders, who received their land directly from the Norman king.

What was the military role of the tenants-in-chief?
Tenants-in-chief had to lead their own army to fight with the king. They were also expected to defend their own land and put down any rebellions there.

How did the tenants-in-chief use their land?
It was up to tenants-in-chief how they used their land to raise an army. With huge fiefdoms, they were integral to the system of land distribution.

How did tenants-in-chief run their fiefs?
A collection of fiefdoms belonging to a tenant-in-chief was called a barony, and each had its own court to sort out disputes.

What role did tenants-in-chief play in the economy?
Tenants-in-chief were very wealthy, even though they passed on some of their revenues to the king.

What political role did the tenants-in-chief play?
Tenants-in-chief sat on the king's council and might give him advice. They also hosted the king and his court when he travelled to their area.

> **DID YOU KNOW?**
> The Earl of Arundel is one of the oldest noble titles in England. The first earl was created in 1138 and the title is currently held by the Duke of Norfolk, who still sits in the House of Lords.

KNIGHTS
Norman power relied on military force, which was represented by the knights.

What were knights in Norman England?
There were an estimated 6,000 knights in Norman England, and they were an important part of the military system in the country.

What was the status of knights in Norman England?
Knights had varying status.
- ☑ Some were granted very little land, or might be retained by a lord as a 'household' knight.
- ☑ Knights replaced thegns as the under-tenants to the tenants-in-chief.

- Many knights were the local lords of the manor.
- They held manor courts to try small disputes among their tenants.

What was the role of knights in Norman England?

Knights had a number of duties in Norman society:

- They were expected to guard the lord's property.
- They had to provide 40 days' military service to the king. This could be to fight in a war, or to garrison a castle in peacetime.
- Rich or powerful knights fought for the king.

What skills did knights have in Norman England?

Knights were extremely well-trained and equipped. They trained as cavalrymen from a very young age.

How were knights used for defence in Norman England?

William needed knights for the defence of England:

- Against the Vikings.
- For wars in Wales and Scotland.
- For wars in France.
- To put down rebellions.
- To garrison castles in order to control the local population.

DID YOU KNOW?

The word 'knight' did not always mean a mounted warrior.

The word knight comes from the Old English word 'cniht', which originally meant 'boy'. The French word for knight is 'chevalier', meaning someone who rides a horse. From this, we get the English word 'cavalier'.

THE NORMAN CHURCH

The Normans used the Church to help them control England. William made significant reforms to the Church in England.

What was the role of the Church in Norman society?

The Church played a key role in Norman society, and the English Church changed as a result of this.

What role did the Norman Church play in the military?

Bishops owed the king military service, so the Church gave land to knights and made sure it could provide soldiers when needed.

What role did the Norman Church play in landholding?

It was a major landholder and owned up to 25% of English land. Church tenants did land service, just as for any other lord, and the Church collected the taxes for the king.

What legal role did the Church play in Norman England?

Because churchmen were among the few literate members of the population, they had an important role to play in the legal system.

- Church clerks wrote the king's royal writs and looked after his seal.
- Bishops sometimes developed laws for the king.
- They advised the king on legal matters.
- The Church organised Trials by Ordeal, where God was given the chance to show the guilt of those accused of crimes.
- William allowed the Church to create its own courts, which dealt with church-related crimes, blasphemy, and legal cases involving marriage.

What political role did the Church play in Norman England?

Important churchmen often paid a key role in William's government.

- Bishops and abbots often acted as William's advisers.
- They sometimes acted as the king's negotiator in important discussions, and as ambassadors to other countries.
- Archbishop Lanfranc stood in for William when he went to Normandy, acting as his regent.

How did the Normans change the Church in England?

The Normans introduced important changes to the Church in England.

- Although many of the priests were still Anglo-Saxon, by 1070 William had replaced all of the important Anglo-Saxon churchmen with Normans.
- In 1070, the Anglo-Saxon Archbishop of Canterbury, Stigand, was replaced by Lanfranc.

What did Lanfranc change about the Norman Church?

Archbishop Lanfranc made many reforms to the Church in England.

- He encouraged William to make the Archbishop of Canterbury the head of the Church in England, securing primacy over the Archbishop of York.
- He also changed several Church rituals.
- Lanfranc tightened up the restrictions on churchmen marrying or having sexual relationships.
- Lanfranc also set up Church courts in 1076 for churchmen who were accused of crimes. This gave the Church a lot of independence from the king, and an important role in the legal system.
- Anglo-Saxon churches were knocked down and rebuilt in the Norman (Romanesque) style, in key locations and market towns.
- Archdeacons - above priests but below bishops - became more and more common.
- Lanfranc, himself an Italian monk, encouraged the revival of monasteries and religious communities.

Why did the Normans change the Norman Church?

William had gained the pope's support for his invasion in 1066 partly because he promised to reform the Church. There were a number of reasons why the Church needed reform.

- There were criticisms of pluralism - clergy holding more than one position, so that they could not effectively fulfil any one role.
- There were criticisms of nepotism - appointing family and friends to positions in the Church, rather than the best men for the job.
- There were criticisms of simony - when positions in the Church were sold to the highest bidder.
- There were also many instances of priests marrying and having children, even though this went against the rules of the Church.

- Stigand, Archbishop of Canterbury, was a prime example of a corrupt priest. This was why William refused to be crowned by Stigand in 1066, because it might cause challenges to his legitimacy.

What was the Normanisation of the English Church in Norman England?
The Normans worked to put their stamp on the Church in England.
- By the 12th century, nearly every Anglo-Saxon church (p.22) building (p.75) had been pulled down and replaced by new buildings in the Norman style.
- Nearly every important Anglo-Saxon churchman had been replaced by a Norman.

How did the Norman Church help keep control for the Normans?
As well as representing Norman ideas, the Church became an effective tool for William to strengthen his hold over England.
- Norman bishops and archbishops encouraged the preaching of positive messages about God's support of William and the Normans.
- With Norman bishops and archbishops, Church land was effectively controlled by the Normans, which helped to prevent rebellions.
- Lanfranc made sure that the Church had more control over priests, which meant that the Anglo-Saxons in the church were more effectively monitored by the Normans.
- New bishops paid homage to the king.
- The king approved Church Council decisions.
- The king appointed new bishops, or replacements for those who died.
- William controlled communication between the English Church and the pope.

CHANGES TO ENGLAND UNDER THE NORMANS
An overview of the main changes that the Normans brought to England.

How much did the Normans change England?
After William conquered England, the Normans kept some things the same, but introduced important changes to English society.

What did the Normans change in England?
The Normans changed a number of important aspects of life in England.
- Government.
- Law Enforcement.
- The use of land and the new forests.
- Taxes and the Domesday Book (p.73).
- The Church.

NORMAN GOVERNMENT

Norman government was a sophisticated regime. William continued with many of the Saxon features of government, as well as introducing some key changes.

What was William's government like in Norman England?
William's government showed a lot of continuity with the Anglo-Saxon government, but he also took opportunities to centralise his power.

What did William keep the same in the Norman government?
William kept a number of important features of Anglo-Saxon government when he took over England.
- ✅ The Anglo-Saxon government was much more sophisticated than the government in Normandy, so William kept many aspects of it when he took over England.
- ✅ The Norman government used the land divisions of 'hides' to work out taxes.
- ✅ They kept the land divisions of shires and hundreds.
- ✅ William still consulted the Witan, or a similar royal council.
- ✅ The Normans still used the silver pennies used by the Anglo-Saxons.
- ✅ The royal treasury remained at Winchester.

How did William limit the power of earls in Norman government?
Edward the Confessor had experienced numerous problems because of the power held by earls such as Godwin. William took the opportunity to limit how much power they could gain.
- ✅ When his loyal followers were replaced, William made their earldoms smaller or, like Wessex and Mercia, redistributed them altogether.
- ✅ The special powers given to the Marcher earls immediately after the invasion were gradually reduced.
- ✅ Earls were tenants-in-chief, and could be punished by forfeiture like other tenants.

How did William use regents in the Norman government?
William had two countries to run, and therefore was absent from either for periods of time. While he was away he appointed regents to keep control in his absence.
- ✅ William's first two regents, Bishop Odo and William FitzOsbern, caused problems and resentment among the Anglo-Saxons in 1067.
- ✅ Archbishop Lanfranc was William's regent in 1075, and helped to prevent the Earls' Revolt *(p.47)*.
- ✅ William often left his wife, Matilda, as regent of Normandy.
- ✅ He tended to return quickly when he heard of problems in England.

DID YOU KNOW?

The way the British government works today has its roots in the Norman system of government. Many aspects of the British Parliament still use words derived from Norman-French.

THE NORMAN SHERIFF
The role of the sheriff in local government in Norman England.

What was a sheriff in Norman England?
The sheriff was the name given to the law enforcement officer who had been known by the Anglo-Saxons as the shire reeve.

What was the job of the sheriff?
William kept the role of the sheriff relatively similar after he took power in England. This role involved:
- ✅ Acting as the king's representative, collecting taxes and looking after the king's personal estates.
- ✅ He administered justice and made sure that the shire met its military obligations.

How did the sheriff's role stay the same?
William kept the sheriff's role more or less the same as it had been in Anglo-Saxon times. However, he replaced the Anglo-Saxons sheriffs with Normans by 1071.
- ✅ Sheriffs were still appointed by the king.
- ✅ The Normans kept the same legal system, with some new punishments for rebellion. *(p.47)*
- ✅ Norman sheriffs continued organising the defence of the shire and gathering men for military service.

How did the sheriff's role change under William?
Some aspects of the sheriff's role changed under William.
- ✅ They were entitled to a share of the taxes that they collected, and could keep the money paid in fines in the shire courts.
- ✅ Sheriffs paid a set sum to the king to collect taxes. Anything they collected above that sum counted as profit.
- ✅ Unlike in Anglo-Saxon times, the sheriff had greater power than the earl in his shire, as he answered directly to the king. Some sheriffs were very powerful and important.
- ✅ Norman sheriffs lost some control when the Church set up its own courts for churchmen in 1076.
- ✅ As well as organising the fyrd, sheriffs were also responsible for overseeing knight *(p.67)* service.
- ✅ Sheriffs were often responsible for the king's castles in the shire.

Why were sheriffs unpopular in Norman England?
Many sheriffs became very unpopular with the Anglo-Saxons. The new Norman laws made it profitable for them to raise taxes for themselves, and they were often involved in land-grabs.

THE ROYAL FORESTS
William and the rest of the Normans were keen on hunting. To satisfy his fondness for it, William created the royal forests and strict laws to accompany them.

What were the Royal Forests?
William kept a bigger area of land for himself ('demesne') than Edward the Confessor had previously. He turned a lot of land into the 'Royal Forests' - land reserved for hunting.

Why did William make the Royal Forests?
William created the Royal Forests because he really enjoyed hunting, particularly deer.

How did William create the Royal Forests?
William confiscated land from other land-holders, including the church, and evicted families from their homes.

What laws covered the Royal Forests?
Numerous laws were created to protect William's hunting grounds and the animals in them.
- ✅ Hunting on private land became a new crime, known as poaching.
- ✅ Damage to the animals or vegetation was prohibited.
- ✅ It was an offence to take weapons or dogs into the forest.
- ✅ It was illegal for ordinary people to hurt the deer, even if the animals were damaging crops.

Why were the Royal Forests important?
The Royal Forests were significant in a number of ways.
- ✅ When William extended his area of land, he legitimised land-grabs being committed by other Normans and made them seem acceptable.
- ✅ It showed the power of the king was greater than the existing law.
- ✅ Harsh punishments for poaching demonstrated Norman ruthlessness.
- ✅ The Anglo-Saxon population began to resent the forests.
- ✅ The forest areas became another source of income for the king.

THE DOMESDAY BOOK

In the 1080s, William set out to create a survey of landholding in England. This became known as the Domesday Survey, or the Domesday Book.

What was the Domesday Book?
The Domesday Book was a survey of England that William commissioned at the end of 1085. It aimed to find out how much was owned by each landholder, and whether they could pay more tax.

Why was the Domesday Book created?
The Domesday Book was produced because William needed to raise more taxes.
- ✅ There was a heavy geld tax in 1084.
- ✅ In 1085 William raised a massive - and expensive - army to defend England against the threat of a Viking invasion (p.37).
- ✅ In 1085, while the Domesday Book was being written, William raised another tax.
- ✅ It may have been a way of getting around the special privileges that meant that many tenants-in-chief didn't have to pay tax on some of their land.

What was in the Domesday Book?
The Domesday Book was a huge document.
- ✅ The Domesday Book was a record of what each landholder owned in each area of England.

- ✅ It was 913 pages long and recorded details of about 1,000 tenants-in-chief and 8,000 under-tenants.
- ✅ It was later called the Domesday Book because the comprehensive information it gathered made people feel as if they had reached the Day of Judgement ('Doomsday').
- ✅ It was written in Latin.

 What was the significance of the Domesday Book?

The Domesday Book was an important document that affected the economy, the military, and the law in Norman England.

 What was the financial significance of the Domesday Book?

The Domesday Book allowed the king and his clerks to see how much money in tax, or relief payments, were owed on each estate.

 What was the legal significance of the Domesday Book?

The Domesday Book was a way of sorting out legal disputes, especially for Anglo-Saxons who claimed to have lost land in land-grabs.

 What was the military significance of the Domesday Book?

The Domesday Book allowed William to see how many soldiers were available if they were needed, for example in response to the Viking threat of 1085.

DID YOU KNOW?

Two facts about the Domesday Survey:
- ✓ There were actually two books, which are kept in the National Archives at Kew, in London.
- ✓ You can look up any place mentioned in the Domesday Survey online - find out who owned the place where you live now back in 1086!

NORMAN CULTURE

The Normans brought great changes to England, introducing elements of their culture, but they borrowed from the Saxons, too.

 What was Norman culture like?

When they moved to England, the Normans aimed to demonstrate their superiority over the Anglo-Saxons by emphasizing their wealth and power.

 What is the definition of Norman culture?

Norman culture was defined by their behaviour and attitudes in important areas, including fashion *(p.75)*, language *(p.77)*, religion, leisure *(p.76)*, and education.

NORMAN FASHION

An overview of Norman fashions.

 What was fashion like in Norman England?
Norman clothing changed after the invasion of England, to reflect their superior status over the Anglo-Saxons.

 How did Norman fashion change after 1066?
Their new status as rulers meant that the Norman fashion changed after the conquest of England in 1066.
- ✅ Before the conquest of England, Norman clothing was very simple and reflected their focus on the army and fighting. After 1066 it became more complicated and elaborate.
- ✅ After 1066, Normans began to incorporate Anglo-Saxon-style embroidery on their clothes.

 What was Norman fashion like for men?
Norman men shaved the back of their heads to demonstrate that they had the luxury of spending time of their appearance. It was also practical, because of the armour they wore on their heads.

NORMAN ARCHITECTURE

The Normans introduced a new style of architecture for castles and churches. This was known as Romanesque.

 What was Norman architecture like?
Norman architecture was often focused on creating the biggest, most imposing and impressive structures possible. New buildings, such as castles and cathedrals, were built in the Romanesque style, brought from the continent.

 How did their conquest of England affect Norman architecture?
One way in which the Normans emphasised their superiority over Anglo-Saxons was through the building of impressive new structures that were bigger and better than anything the Anglo-Saxons had.
- ✅ By the 12th century, every Anglo-Saxon cathedral and church had been demolished and rebuilt by the Normans in the Romanesque style.
- ✅ Norman buildings tended to be larger than any Anglo-Saxon buildings. Westminster Great Hall, for example, was the largest hall in Europe.

 What did Norman architecture look like?
The new Norman architecture was known as Romanesque. It used features that reminded people of the architecture of the Roman empire, hence its name.
- ✅ The overall impression was of size and grandeur. Romanesque buildings were much larger than anything the Saxons had been able to build.
- ✅ The Romanesque style was characterised by thick walls, round arches, sturdy pillars, and symmetry.
- ✅ Ceilings were vaulted, which allowed the interior to be much higher than in earlier buildings.
- ✅ Decorations seemed complex, but were made up of simple patterns such as chevrons and herring-bones.

> **DID YOU KNOW?**
>
> **Three facts about Romanesque castles and cathedrals:**
> - ✔ Early stone-built castles employed Romanesque architecture. Examples include the Tower of London, Colchester Castle, and Rochester Castle.
> - ✔ Durham Cathedral was one of earliest Romanesque cathedrals.
> - ✔ Building cathedrals took such a long time that many incorporated Gothic features by the time they were completed.

NORMAN LEISURE

Norman lords had more leisure time as they had Saxon peasants to do all the work.

What did the Normans like to do for leisure?
The Normans enjoyed hunting. They had complicated procedures to butcher their meat, showing they had leisure time to spare.

NORMAN CHIVALRY

The Normans were militaristic and developed sophisticated rules of conduct for warfare.

What was chivalry in Norman times?
Normans placed a lot of emphasis on chivalry, which focused on knights and the 'correct' way to engage in battle.

NORMAN CHRISTIANITY

The Normans were very religious and took their observances seriously.

What was religion like in Norman times?
The Normans were Christian and very religious, but also very violent and focused on warfare. They reconciled this by doing 'penance', praying and building *(p.75)* churches to gain forgiveness for their sins.

NORMAN ATTITUDES TO THE ANGLO-SAXONS

England had become divided, with the majority of the population remaining Anglo-Saxon while the rulers and nobles were mostly Norman or French.

What did the Normans think of the Anglo-Saxons?

The Norman aristocracy considered themselves far superior to the Anglo-Saxons, and were often insulting towards and about them.

CHANGES TO INHERITANCE LAWS UNDER THE NORMANS

William made major changes to the rules by which people could inherit land in England.

How did the Normans change inheritance?

The Anglo-Saxons traditionally divided the estates of a dead man amongst his sons. This meant that estates became smaller and smaller, and sometimes led to conflict between family members. The Normans changed inheritance laws.

What did the Normans change about inheritance law?

The Normans made five important changes to inheritance.

- ☑ The Normans introduced male primogeniture, where the eldest son inherited all the lands of the father. This helped to keep estates intact.
- ☑ When a man died without an heir his lands returned to the lord, who could keep it or grant it to another of his followers.
- ☑ If an heir was under-age, the lord took over the land until the heir was of age. He could enjoy the revenue of the land until that time.
- ☑ Widows came under the control of the lord or king. He could arrange a new marriage for her, often to one of his followers, who then gained the land.
- ☑ If the deceased only had daughters, they came under the control of the lord or king. He could arrange their marriage to one of his followers, who then gained the land.

> **DID YOU KNOW?**
>
> The Norman inheritance law of male primogeniture was used in the succession to the throne right up to 2015. It was abolished in case the Duke and Duchess of Cambridge's first child was a girl.

THE NORMAN LANGUAGE

The Normans even changed the use of language in England.

What language did the Normans speak?

The Normans spoke a form of French, known as Norman-French, which was an additional barrier between them and the English.

Could the Normans speak the English language?

With the Norman conquest, the language of the Anglo-Saxons became less important.

- English was only spoken by the common people, and only survived as a written language in a few places.
- William tried to learn English, but gave it up because he didn't have the time.
- Archbishop Lanfranc couldn't speak English.
- As time went on, more Normans learnt to speak both languages, and some Anglo-Saxons - such as Hereward the Wake - could speak French.

What was the official language in Norman England?

Under the Normans, English declined as the spoken language in certain areas, and it almost completely disappeared as a written language. Norman-French and Latin became the official languages.

- Norman French was the language of the king's court, and was the language used by the upper classes. It was also used for teaching.
- Over time, Norman-French developed into Anglo-Norman, as some English words were adopted.
- Under Norman rule, English disappeared from government and the Church. Latin became the language of government and the Church.
- Latin was also the language used by merchants who travelled overseas, as it was the language that all educated people in Europe spoke.

DID YOU KNOW?

It is estimated around 46% of words in the English language are derived from Norman-French.

GLOSSARY

A

Abbot, Abbots - the male head of a monastery or leader of a group of monks.

Allegiance - loyalty to a person, group or cause.

Alliance - a union between groups or countries that benefits each member.

Allies - parties working together for a common objective, such as countries involved in a war. In both world wars, 'Allies' refers to those countries on the side of Great Britain.

Ambassador - someone, often a diplomat, who represents their state, country or organisation in a different setting or place.

Archbishop, Archbishops - a chief bishop in the Christian church, responsible for a major area.

Archer - someone who uses a bow and arrow; usually refers to those who used bows in warfare.

Aristocracy - the highest social class, whose members gain their power from possessing land, property and money.

Assassination - the act of murdering someone, usually an important person.

Autonomy - independence or self-government.

B

Barracks - a military building, or group of buildings, housing soldiers.

Bishop, Bishops - a senior member of the Christian Church, usually in charge of a diocese.

Blasphemy - the act of speaking insultingly about or with lack of reverence for God or sacred objects.

Boon work - the work a peasant did on his lord's land, usually for two or three days a week, often in lieu of paying rent for the peasant's own land.

Bribe, Bribery, Bribes - to dishonestly persuade someone to do something for you in return for money or other inducements.

Burh, Burhs - a fortified town in Anglo-Saxon England. There was at least one in each shire. The law stated all trading over a certain amount had to take place in the burh so it could be taxed.

C

Campaign - a political movement to get something changed; in military terms, it refers to a series of operations to achieve a goal.

Cathedral, Cathedrals - the principal church in a diocese, with which a bishop is associated.

Cavalry - the name given to soldiers who fight on horseback.

Celibacy - the state of being celibate.

Ceorl - a peasant who was free to leave their lord's land to seek work elsewhere, sometimes known as a freeman.

Charter - a legal written grant, issued by a monarch or country's legislative power, permitting certain rights or privileges.

Claim - someone's assertion of their right to something - for example, a claim to the throne.

Clergy - those ordained for religious duties, especially in the Christian Church.

Collective responsibility - when a group of people is held responsible for an action or outcome, regardless of anyone's individual behaviour or performance.

Consolidate - to strengthen a position, often politically, by bringing several things together into a more effective whole.

Coronation - the ceremony of crowning a monarch.

Corrupt - when someone is willing to act dishonestly for their own personal gain.

Council - an advisory or administrative body set up to manage the affairs of a place or organisation. The Council of the League of Nations contained the organisation's most powerful members.

Counterfeit - a fake or fraudulent imitation, intended to deceive someone into believing it is genuine.

Counterfeiting - the act of producing a fake or fraudulent imitation of something.

Culture - the ideas, customs, and social behaviour of a particular people or society.

Currency - an umbrella term for any form of legal tender, but most commonly referring to money.

D

Demesne - land owned and retained under the direct control of a lord rather than leased out to a sub-tenant.

Deploy - to move military troops or equipment into position or a place so they are ready for action.

Destrier - a Norman war horse, bred and trained to be strong and vicious in battle.

Dispute - a disagreement or argument; often used to describe conflict between different countries.

E

Earl, Earls - the most important men in the country after the monarch during medieval times.

Earldom - area of land governed by an earl or high-ranking noble.

Economic - relating to the economy; also used when justifying something in terms of profitability.

Economy - a country, state or region's position in terms of production and consumption of goods and services, and the supply of money.

Embassy - historically, a deputation sent by one ruler, state or country to another. More recently, it is also the accepted name for the official residence or offices of an ambassador.

Empire - a group of states or countries ruled over and controlled by a single monarch.

GLOSSARY

Encircle, Encirclement - a military term for enemy forces isolating and surrounding their target.

Estate, Estates - an extensive area of land, usually in the country and including a large house. It tends to be owned by one person, family or organisation.

Excommunicate, Excommunication - to formally expel someone from the Catholic Church. Someone who is excommunicated is forbidden from participating in sacraments and services, and often believes their soul is condemned.

Exile - to be banned from one's original country, usually as a punishment or for political reasons.

F

Famine - a severe food shortage resulting in starvation and death, usually the result of bad harvests.

Fasting - to deliberately refrain from eating, and often drinking, for a period of time.

Feudal - relating to the feudal system.

Fief - an area or estate held by a vassal as part of the feudal system in medieval England.

Front - in war, the area where fighting is taking place.

Frontier - a line or border between two areas.

Fyrd - an army that could be raised by the king if needed to fight in Anglo-Saxon England. Every five hides had to provide a man to fight in the fyrd for a maximum of 40 days.

G

Guerrilla tactics, Guerrilla warfare - a way of fighting that typically involves hit-and-run style tactics.

Guerrillas - groups of small, independent fighters usually involved in a war against larger, regular military forces.

H

Harvest - the process of gathering and collecting crops.

Heir - someone who is entitled to property or rank following the current owner or holder's death.

Hide - a measurement of land in Saxon times, equivalent to around 120 acres.

Hierarchies, Hierarchy - the ranking of people according to authority, for example a colonel in the army being higher than a corporal.

Homage - to demonstrate allegiance or respect to another in public.

I

Illegitimate - the term given to a child born to unmarried parents; generally, not authorised by law.

Independence, Independent - to be free of control, often meaning by another country, allowing the people of a nation the ability to govern themselves.

Industry - the part of the economy concerned with turning raw materials into into manufactured goods, for example making furniture from wood.

Infantry - soldiers who march and fight on foot.

Interpretation, Interpretations - a perceived meaning or particular explanation of something.

L

Lance, Lanced, Lancing - to prick or cut open something, such as an abscess, and let it drain.

Lease, Leases - a contract granting the use of something such as land or property for a specified period of time, usually in return for payment.

Legitimacy, Legitimate - accepted by law or conforming to the rules; can be defended as valid.

Literate - someone who can read and write.

Lord, Lords - a man of high status, wealth and authority.

M

Mass - an act of worship in the Catholic Church.

Mercenary - someone who takes action in order to earn money, rather than out of principle.

Merchant, Merchants - someone who sells goods or services.

Military force - the use of armed forces.

Monasteries, Monastery - a religious building occupied by monks.

Monk - a member of a religious community, often living a simple life of poverty, chastity and work.

Morale - general mood of a group of people.

N

Nepotism - the practice of people in power favouring friends and family, often by giving them jobs or influence. Historically, this was especially common in government and the Church.

Nobility - the social class ranked directly below royalty.

Noble, Nobles - another word for aristocrat - a member of the highest and richest class in society.

O

Oath - a solemn promise with special significance, often relating to future behaviour or actions.

P

Peasant - a poor farmer.

Penance - a punishment willingly undertaken or inflicted on

GLOSSARY

oneself to show sorrow and repentance for committing a sin, and to gain forgiveness.

Pious - devoutly religious.

Pluralism - the practice, especially in the church, of holding more than one job at a time. There was concern that a person could not do any job properly because their attention was divided.

Pope - the head of the Roman Catholic Church.

Population - the number of people who live in a specified place.

Pragmatic - taking a practical approach; being sensible and realistic.

Predecessor - the person who came before; the previous person to fill a role or position.

Prevent, Preventative, Preventive - steps taken to stop something from happening.

Proclamation - a public or official announcement of great importance.

Production - a term used to describe how much of something is made, for example saying a factory has a high production rate.

Profit - generally refers to financial gain; the amount of money made after deducting buying, operating or production costs.

R

Raid - a quick surprise attack on the enemy.

Rallies, Rally - a political event with speakers and a crowd, designed to increase support for a politician, political party or an idea.

Rebellion - armed resistance against a government or leader, or resistance to other authority or control.

Rebels - people who rise in opposition or armed resistance against an established government or leader.

Reform, Reforming - change, usually in order to improve an institution or practice.

Refugee, Refugees - a person who has been forced to leave where they live due to war, disaster or persecution.

Regent - the person who rules when the king is away, incapacitated or too young to rule.

Reign - a period of power, usually by a monarch.

Repent, Repented, Repenting - to feel or express remorse and regret for one's wrongdoings or sins.

Romanesque - a style of architecture from the final period of the Roman Empire.

S

Secular - unconnected to religious or spiritual matters; not bound by religious rule.

Sheriff, Sheriffs - an important royal official in medieval England, responsible for running the local court and ensuring tax was paid to the monarch.

Shield wall - a highly effective battle tactic where soldiers would stand in a row with their shields overlapping.

Shire - a defined area of land in England during the Saxon and medieval periods, later known as a county.

Siege - action by enemy forces to surround a place or building, cutting off access and supplies, with the aim of either destroying it, gaining entry, or starving the inhabitants out.

Simony - the practice, especially in the church, of selling offices or roles rather than appointing people on their merits.

Sin - in religion, an immoral act against God's laws.

State, States - an area of land or a territory ruled by one government.

Strategy - a plan of action outlining how a goal will be achieved.

Strike - a refusal by employees to work as a form of protest, usually to bring about change in their working conditions. It puts pressure on their employer, who cannot run the business without workers.

Submission, Submit - a formal surrender and acceptance of a new authority.

Successor - someone who succeeds the previous person, such as a leader who takes over the role from the previous holder.

Superior - better or higher in rank, status or quality.

T

Tactic - a strategy or method of achieving a goal.

Tenant-In-chief, Tenants-In-chief - a person who controlled land leased to them by the monarch.

Territories, Territory - an area of land under the control of a ruler/country.

The crown, The throne - phrases used to represent royal power. For example, if someone 'seizes the throne' it means they have taken control. Can also refer to physical objects.

Thegn - the local lord in Anglo-Saxon times, a wealthy and important man. Thegns owned more than 5 hides of land and rented it out to peasants.

Treason - the crime of betraying one's country, often involving an attempt to overthrow the government or kill the monarch.

Treasury - a place or building where money or treasure is held; also refers to a government department related to finance and taxation.

U

Upper class - a socio-economic group consisting of the richest people in a society who are wealthy because they own land or property.

V

Vassal - someone who held their land in return for service and was expected to swear oaths of homage and fealty to their lord.

GLOSSARY

Villein - an unfree peasant, tied to the land where he lived and unable to leave without his lord's permission.

Voyage - a long journey involving travel by sea or in space.

W

Wergild - meaning 'man price', this was the value placed on a man's life in Saxon England and the amount of compensation to be paid for his injury or death.

Writ - a written command from a court or other legal authority.

INDEX

A

Aelfgar - *26*
Anglo-Saxon
    Church - *22*
    Economy - *21*
    King - *16*
    Land - *18*
    Law enforcement - *19*
    Power - *17*
    Rebellions against William I - *47*
    Soldier - *19*
    Surrender after Hastings - *42*
    Wergild - *20*
Anglo-Saxons - *14*
Architecture - *75*
Armies at the Battle of Hastings - *41*
Army, Anglo-Saxon - *19*

B

Battle of Gate Fulford - *36*
Battle of Hastings - *38*
Battle of Hastings, armies - *41*
Battle of Stamford Bridge - *36*
Bishop Odo - *61*
    Rebellion against William Rufus - *61*
    Relationship with William I - *61*

C

Castles, Norman - *45*
Changes, Norman - *70*
Chivalry - *76*
Church, Anglo-Saxon - *22*
Church, Norman - *68*
Confessor, Edward - *23*
Contenders to the throne, 1066 - *27*
Culture - *74*
Curthose, Robert - *59*

D

Danelaw - *16*
Domesday Book - *73*
Domesday Survey - *73*

E

Earl Godwin - *24*
Earls' Revolt, 1075 - *53*
East Anglian revolt, 1071 - *52*
Economy, Anglo-Saxon - *21*
Edgar Aetheling - *34*
    Claim to throne - *34*
    Coronation - *35*
    Rebellion - *35*
Edgar Aetheling rebellion, 1069 - *49*
Edward the Confessor - *23*
    and Normandy - *23*
Edwin and Morcar, rebellion - *47*

F

Fashion - *75*
Feudal System - *65*
    Exchanges - *66*
    Forfeiture - *66*

G

Gate Fulford, Battle of - *36*
Godwin - *24*
    Exile - *24*
    Family - *25*
    Power - *24*
    Rivals - *25*
    Role in England - *24*
    and Edward the Confessor - *24*
Government, Norman - *71*

H

Harald Hardrada - *33*
    Battles - *34*
    Claim to throne - *33*
Harold Godwinson - *29*
    Actions as king - *31*
    Battles - *31*
    Challenges - *31*
    Claim to throne - *30*
    Coronation - *31*
    Death - *33*
    Family - *29*
    Oath to William - *30*

INDEX

    Visit to Normandy - 29
    and Tostig - 29
    at Battle of Hastings - 32
Harrying of the North, 1069-70 - 51
Hastings, Battle of - 38
Henry I
    Accession - 61
Hereward the Wake rebellion, 1071 - 52

I

Inheritance - 77

K

King, Anglo-Saxon - 16
Knights - 67

L

Land, Anglo-Saxon - 18
Landholding, Norman - 64
Language - 77
Law enforcement, Anglo-Saxon - 19
Leisure - 76

M

Marcher earldoms - 44
Motte and Bailey castles - 45

N

Norman
    Architecture - 75
    Castles - 45
    Changes - 70
    Chivalry - 76
    Church - 68
    Culture - 74
    Fashion - 75
    Government - 71
    Inheritance - 77
    Knights - 67
    Language - 77
    Leisure - 76
    Redistribution of land - 62
    Religion - 76
    Tenants-in-chief - 67

    Threat to England, 1066 - 38
    Views of Anglo-Saxons - 77
    landholding - 64

O

Odo of Bayeux - 61

P

Population of England, 1060 - 14
Power, Anglo-Saxon - 17

R

Rebellion
    Earls' Revolt, 1075 - 53
    East Anglia - 52
    Edgar Aetheling - 49
    Edwin and Morcar, 1068 - 47
    Hereward the Wake - 52
Rebellions
    against William I - 47
Redistribution of land, Norman - 62
Religion, Norman - 76
Revolt against Tostig - 26
Robert Curthose - 59
    Rebellion against William Rufus - 59
    Relationship with William I - 59
Royal forest - 72

S

Sheriff, role of - 72
Significance of Viking defeat, 1066 - 37
Soldier, Anglo-Saxon - 19
Stamford Bridge, Battle of - 36
Succession crisis, 1066 - 27

T

Tenants-in-chief - 67
Tostig revolt - 26

V

Viking defeat, significance - 37
Viking invasion of England, 1066 - 35

W

INDEX

Wergild, Anglo-Saxon - *20*

William I
    Claim to throne - *55*
    Coronation - *57*
    Death - *58*
    Family - *58*
    Military power - *57*
    Personality - *58*
    Power - *57*
    Rewards to followers - *43*
    Writs - *58*
    at Battle of Hastings - *55*

William I - *55*

William II - *60*

William Rufus
    Challenge to rule - *60*
    Rebellions - *60*
    Succession - *59*
    and Robert Curthose - *60*

William Rufus - *60*

William the Conqueror - *55*